YELLOW

CLEVELAND

THE MAN OF PEACE

CLARK KENT

Yellow Cleveland – The Man of Peace © 2016 by Clark Kent.

All rights reserved. Printed in the United States of America. No part of this book may be used or reproduced in any manner whatsoever without written permission except in the case of brief quotations embodied in critical articles or reviews.

This book is a work of partial-fiction. However, names, characters, businesses, organizations, places, events and incidents either are the product of the author's imagination or are used fictitiously. Any resemblance to actual persons, living or dead, events, or locales is entirely coincidental.

For information contact: info@uptownmediaventures.com

Book and Cover design by Team Uptown

ISBN: 978-1-68121-036-0

First Edition: March 2016

10 9 8 7 6 5 4 3 2 1

I dedicate this book to the loving memory of my father. May you rest in peace until the Day of Judgment.

In Memory of

Robert Joel Gaines (Addul Salaam)

7/10/1949 - 11/14/2015

Page left intentionally blank

Table of Contents

Chapter	Page
1 The Funeral	7
2 The Reunion	17
3 Scape Goat	25
4 The Set Up	33
5 The Light in the Darkness	43
6 Ready Set Go	53
7 Footprints	65
8 Que Sera Sera	75
9 Easy Like Sunday Morning	85
10 Road Trip	95
11 Coming Home	105
12 Grace and Forgiveness	113
13 Loose Ends	121
14 Dirty Laundry	127

CLARK KENT

Chapter	Page
15 Meeting the Brothers	133
16 Cruising Through the City	141
17 The Change	149
About the Author	155

Chapter 1
The Funeral

I will never forget the day that we buried my best friend and cousin Smooth, and his girl Diamond. It was a double funeral. The night before the funeral there were so many people that there was a line out the door just for the viewing. The parking lot looked like a car show. Cars with custom paint jobs and fancy rims lined the street of the funeral parlor. It seemed like every pimp, every player, and every other hustler from Hollywood to Long Beach showed up to pay condolences to their fallen soldiers.

Smooth and Diamond were the real definition of hustlers. They refused to let one game define their hustle. They were more like the jacks of all trades when it came to getting money. They were known to have worked just about every street hustle there was. They had to have been the most well known couple ever to have a funeral together. As nice as it sounds, it was by far the saddest funeral I had ever been to.

CLARK KENT

Diamond's autopsy had revealed that she was three months pregnant. She had been taking classes at the community college and wanted to quit the life. Smooth had planned to use the money from the diamond heist to get out of the game. Uncle Jimmy had set it up for Smooth and Diamond to move to Santa Ana and manage an apartment building.

At the time I was totally unaware of what his plans had been when he came to Vegas. All I knew was that he had been casing some hustle or another in Vegas. I hadn't even expected him to show up in Vegas while I was there. I knew that I had joked with him about meeting up in Vegas, but I never really counted on him showing up.

Sitting in front of his closed casket brought back memories of us throughout life. I thought about when we were kids before he had moved to California. When we first tried out for the East 97th street Bulldogs. Smooth had made the starting team. He was taller and a lot faster than I was. When the coach threatened to cut me from the team Smooth told the coach that if I couldn't play, he wasn't either.

The coach had given Smooth the starting quarterback position; it was no secret that Smooth was definitely the team leader. He had charisma; he also knew how to make people do what he told them to. So when he threatened to quit, the coaches decided to put me on the special team's squad just to keep him on the team.

I thought about when Smooth had stomped out the pimp who had disrespected Jersey the night she had died. My eyes began to water up and tears started to form in my eyes causing my vision to blur. The line was still out of the door for people to pay their last respects. As people walked past the two closed caskets they kissed the pictures of Smooth and Diamond that were on easels in front of the caskets.

A slideshow of pictures played on a screen at the front of the funeral parlor. Pictures of Diamond as a young girl flashed followed by pictures of Smooth dressed for prom. As the pictures changed it seem to serve as a reminder of just how quickly life could be taken away. I thought about when I had gone to jail trying to make money for picking Diamond up from a hotel. I remembered how I had thought that Smooth and Diamond had set me up. My mind flashed to the pictures of Jersey that the detective had forced me to look at.

CLARK KENT

Her throat was cut and her eyes seemed to be looking right at me, begging me to help her. I remembered how the next picture they had showed me was of her body, and all of the stab wounds. It hurt me to think that I was supposed to be her protector. I called myself her pimp, yet I hadn't even prevented her death. More tears began to run from my eyes as the beautiful voice of a young boy sang: *"This songs dedicated to my homies, in that gangster lean..."*

I looked up and saw that Bishop Don was walking up to the caskets. He was wearing one of his signature green and gold suits. As he approached the caskets he stopped and took off his hat. He said something quietly and proceeded towards the rows of chairs looking for a place to sit.

Pretty Tony walked up to the caskets wearing a black suit with four of his girls all dressed in black with veils. Each of the girls placed a dozen roses by the caskets and then walked with Pretty Tony to hug Smooth's mother. I stood up and he gave me a hug but didn't say a word. He had tears in his eyes and it was plain to see that he felt the loss just as much if not more than any of us.

YELLOW CLEVELAND – The Man of Peace

After almost an hour the last of the people walking up to pay there respects ended and the funeral parlor was full. I sat there with my head down looking at the floor. Memories flashed through my mind of Smooth and I at different points of our lives.

I thought about when he had gotten caught stealing candy when we were kids. Smooth had taken the blame and said that he had put the candy in my pocket. He was on punishment for a week and never changed his story. Smooth had always had my back.

I thought about when I had first showed up in Hollywood greener than a blade of grass and how he had showed me the way to work the California streets. He had introduced me to all of the other hustlers and pimps, and had everybody looking out for me. My eyes began to water up to the point that I could no longer see. Tears started to roll down my cheeks.

Over the speaker system I heard a voice that was very familiar. As I sat with my head in my hands listening I realized whose voice it was. It was my big brother Darryl. I wiped my eyes and sat up looking at the front of the funeral parlor. Darryl was wearing the robe of a preacher. He had on glasses and looked like a real minister.

CLARK KENT

The Darryl I remembered was the last person you would expect to see dressed as a preacher much less actually being a preacher. As he spoke he made countless references to bible passages. There was no doubt that somehow my big brother had become a minister. After he spoke he came and sat beside me while a few other people spoke to the crowd about Smooth and Diamond.

A girl sang *"I'll be missing you"* as the funeral director lead us to the front of the room to carry the caskets out to the hearses. Twelve of us stood and walked to the front of the room. At the front of the room we split into teams of six and carried the caskets out of the funeral home. After we put them into the hearses I turned and walked to my car. Darryl caught up with me and I stopped to hug him.

"It's been way too long bro," he said as we started to walk.

"Big brother! Wow man, what in the hell happened to you?" I asked.

"It's funny that you chose those words to ask that question, because the question just answered itself," he said as we approached my car.

"What is that supposed to mean bro?" I asked.

YELLOW CLEVELAND – The Man of Peace

"Everything in Hell that happened to me caused me to give up and give my life to Christ," he said.

"Look bro, if you're going to be trying to preach to me now is not the right time," I said.

"Look bro I'm just glad to see you. That's all," he said as he walked over to the passenger side of the car.

"Get in nigga let's roll," I told him.

As I began to unlock the doors I noticed a detective's car with two detectives parked across the street watching as people came out to their cars for the funeral procession. One of the detectives was holding a pair of binoculars; the other detective appeared to be writing on a small tablet.

"These punk ass cops can't even let a nigga die in peace," I said as I gave him the finger. I was sure that he was writing down license plate numbers and taking pictures of every person and every car in the procession. They would have a lot of work to do because there was no way that two police officers could run the plates of all of the cars that had showed up.

As we stood watching the police who were watching the funeral procession I wondered why they had even come to the funeral. I was sure there were countless

CLARK KENT

unsolved murders that needed to be worked on. Jersey had been murdered and was still a cold case. The murder rate was rising every day and yet here I was watching two police waste their time standing around at a funeral.

A metallic blue Cadillac with gold rims rolled past on three wheels blasting its radio. As they rolled past the detectives the car started bouncing up and down as the driver put a hand out of the window giving the detectives the middle finger. Obviously I wasn't the only person who was offended by their presence.

As we stood there looking at all of the people coming out of the funeral, an older guy who was decked out in a blue paisley outfit and another big guy wearing an all black suit and a Godfather hat, walked over to us. I noticed T and B right away. T was representing the Crips hard, he was even wearing glasses with paisley designs.

"What up Cuz?" said B as he walked over and gave me a hug. "If you need anything… Anything! You know how to reach me," He said as he raised his shirt and showed his pistol.

"Yeah, I'll be in touch," I told him as I unlocked the doors to the car. I already knew what he meant. They walked away and walked in the direction of the parking lot.

YELLOW CLEVELAND – The Man of Peace

I looked back across the street and saw the detective looking at me through binoculars. I shook my head and laughed. The funny thing was that it would be hard to find a person who wasn't wanted at this funeral. I opened the door and hit the lock button and looked back at the hearse. It was my cousins last ride.

Chapter 2

The Reunion

We got into the car and waited for everyone else in the procession to pull off. Once we were in the car I looked at my brother and shook my head. As I sat in the car I noticed that it had started to drizzle. The sun was bright yet it was raining.

"Look lil bro, I'm sorry about what happened to Charles and his girl. I pray for their souls, but I really need to reach out to you. Nobody hears from you anymore, you're out here doing God knows what and we never know when we're going to get the call that it's you dead," Darryl said as we began to pull off.

"Bro please! I told you I wasn't in the mood for all that preacher game right now. If that's what you rode with me for you're wasting your time," I said.

"My fault bro. How are you though?" he asked.

"I'm holdin' up. You know getting paid like you used to my nigga," I said.

CLARK KENT

"That's what worries me man, but we ain't gotta talk about that right now," he said. As we drove, a rainbow formed over the street. I thought about how Smooth was always chasing money. Now the rainbow almost made it appear that he had finally made it to the end of the rainbow and maybe he had found his pot of gold after all. I turned on the radio and *"I aint mad at ya"* by Tupac was playing.

We rode in silence listening to the radio until we turned into the graveyard. I turned off the radio as we approached the entrance. The cars snaked their way through the graveyard until they stopped at a gravesite with a green tent over it. My thoughts drifted to being in church with my family when I was younger. I could almost feel my sister sitting next to me trying her best to stay awake but loosing the battle as the preacher gave his sermon.

I parked the car and got out to carry the casket to the gravesite. Before I started walking I reached into my pocket and pulled out a small bottle of Hennessy that I had bought on my way to the funeral. I opened it and poured out half of the bottle in memory of Smooth and Diamond. I downed the rest and tossed the bottle into the bushes. I walked to the hearse and waited for them to open the back door.

YELLOW CLEVELAND – The Man of Peace

As we carried the caskets to the gravesite I felt the sting of loosing my best friend once again. We placed the caskets over the gravesites and stepped back as my brother said the final words before they lowered the caskets into the ground. I put the first shovel of dirt over Smooth's casket and passed the shovel to the person behind me. I walked away from the gravesite and stood under a tree.

I thought about all of the things that had led me to California. I envisioned myself in Junior High school fighting to be accepted by the rest of the black kids in school. I thought about when I had gotten beaten up by the white police and thrown out of the car at the lake. I could still remember the look on Tone's face when he gained conciseness.

I pulled a blunt out of my pocket that I had rolled to smoke after the funeral. I lit it and inhaled as much smoke as I could bear. "This is for you cuzzo," I said as I exhaled the smoke. I stood there watching the crowd of people gathered around the side by side graves of Smooth and Diamond. I finished the blunt and tossed the roach into the grass.

"You cool little bro?" Darryl said as he walked up.

CLARK KENT

"I'm bout cool as I can be considering the circumstances," I said as I turned to face him. It had been years since I had seen my big brother. On top of that he was a preacher now. I wondered what I had missed that caused things to turn out like this.

"Look bro I know you don't want to hear a bunch of preaching, but I need you to know that the family has been praying for you. Mom and Pops have been worried to death about you being out here," Darryl said as we began to walk to the car.

"Bro I'm good! Y'all act like because I dropped out of school that I'm some sort of failure. I've been getting money since I was a kid. Shit they kicked me out, what was I supposed to do? And you... You come out here dressed like a preacher, but the last time I saw you, you were playing me out of money from the weed I fronted you," I said.

"What? How the fuck can you say that? I'm the one who paid for that girl's abortion! I'm the only reason you even started getting money nigga! Have you forgotten that you didn't even know how to weigh the shit up? The only reason you even made anything off of that weed was because of me. So don't give me that bullshit about I played you out of some money, which by the way wasn't

YELLOW CLEVELAND – The Man of Peace

even yours," Darryl said as he opened the car door. I got into the drivers seat and closed the door.

At first I didn't speak. I started the car up and turned on the radio. As I pulled off I took one last look at the funeral site. I didn't want to socialize with anyone or even hear any of their conversations. Hell for that matter I really wasn't even in the mood to be riding with my brother right now.

I decided to drive out to Newport Beach to meet up with Uncle Jimmy. I knew he would get a kick out of seeing Darryl. He hadn't come to the funeral because he said there might be some people who thought it was his fault that Smooth and Diamond were dead. He had been at the viewing of the bodies and left big wreaths of flowers the night before.

"So how long will you be in our lovely state bro?" I asked after the silence started to become uncomfortable.

"Well, that depends on you bro," he said as we pulled into traffic. I could tell from the way he had said it that he had an agenda. As a matter of fact I knew that with Darryl there was always a hidden agenda.

"How does the length of your stay end up having anything to do with me?" I asked.

CLARK KENT

"I came out here to bring you home. It's time to stop running from your problems and get back home. Mama and Pops asked me to come out here and talk to you," he said as he pulled a pack of Newport's out of his jacket pocket.

"Big bro Cleveland hasn't been my home in years. As far as running goes I was never running from anything. I left to get away from all of the bullshit," I told him.

As we rode I thought about how much had happened since I first arrived in Cali. I thought about all of the money and connections I had made. I was definitely going to miss my cousin.

"Mind if I smoke?" he asked as he lit his cigarette. When I rolled down the window the smell of the ocean reminded me of the peace of mind I always felt at the beaches. We got off of the freeway at Newport Beach blvd. We turned onto Balboa where the traffic became congested, moving at almost a snails pace. After almost twenty minutes of stop and go traffic we found a parking space in front of The District, a 100 year old bar right near the beach. We got out and walked into the bar. When we sat at the bar I looked at Darryl and started to laugh. The bartender walked over and asked us what we

YELLOW CLEVELAND – The Man of Peace

would like to drink. I told her that first she had to bring me one of the t- shirts that had the logo of the bar.

"Big bro you gotta take that shirt and collar off! You got people lookin at us like we some kind of circus act. I don't even think preachers are allowed in here," I said as she walked away. When she came back I ordered a pitcher of beer and Darryl ordered a glass of orange juice. Darryl asked her where the restrooms were and went to change shirts.

I pulled out my phone and called Uncle Jimmy. He answered on the first ring and told me that he was across the street at the Newport Beach Marina getting something from his yacht and that he couldn't wait to see Darryl. I hung up the phone and sipped my beer. The last time I had come here I was with Smooth coming to meet up with Uncle Jimmy. The District was one of Jimmy's favorite hangouts. It was also where he did most of his business.

My mind flashed to a time that I had brought Jersey here pick up money from one of Jimmy's workers. I was snapped back to reality as Darryl came out wearing the T-shirt and a gold herring bone necklace with a cross hanging from it.

CLARK KENT

"Damn bro you went from preacher to pimp," I said as he sat down. Now he looked more like the Darryl I remembered. "Are you sure you don't want a drink bro? I won't tell anybody," I said as I slid a glass of beer to him. He reluctantly took the beer and we sat talking about old times. I ordered two shots of Hennessy and we toasted to the memory of Smooth and Diamond.

Chapter 3

Scape Goat

Uncle Jimmy walked in and stood by the bar and whispered something to the waitress then came over to our table. Darryl stood up and gave him a hug. A waitress showed up carrying a tray of drinks.

"Boy you sure are a sight for sore eyes. I heard that you gave a wonderful sermon at the funeral. Lord knows most of the people there needed to hear it," Uncle Jimmy said as he sat down.

"Thank you Unc, it was hard to do but with the grace of God I got it done," Darryl said as he sipped his beer.

"Yeah I definitely couldn't have gotten up there, it was hard enough just being there," I said as I downed the rest of my beer.

"This is 50 year old scotch from Ireland. I brought this bottle from my personal collection. I had it chilled to give it the perfect taste. Fella's this is in memory of my nephew," Uncle Jimmy said as his eyes began to tear up. We downed the shots and sat in silence for a minute. I

CLARK KENT

stood up and told Jimmy I was going out to smoke. I walked out and let Darryl and Jimmy do some catching up. I needed some air.

As I walked to the entrance of the bar I noticed a black S.U.V. with tinted windows parked out in front of the bar. As I continued walking two men dressed in dark suits got out of the S.U.V. The bouncer who usually stood at the entrance to the bar had gone inside and there was no one other than the two men from the S.U.V. in front of the bar.

My first thought was to turn around and walk back to the table. Against my better judgment I walked out to the front of the bar and lit a cigarette. The two men who had gotten out of the S.U.V. walked over to me and kind of boxed me in.

"Got an extra smoke my man?" the shorter of the two asked as the bigger guy closed in on me and cornered me in.

"Naw bro, this motherfuckin pack only had twenty. I ain't get any extra ones in this pack, how about yours?" I asked with a smirk on my face. The bigger guy grabbed me up by my collar. He pushed me against the building. The shorter guy walked over and waved the big guy off of me.

YELLOW CLEVELAND – The Man of Peace

"Look asshole! I'm only going to say this once. You got something that doesn't belong to you and no matter what I have to do to you to make you give it back to me; I am more than ready to do it," he screamed as he pulled out a silver pistol and jabbed me in the ribs with it.

I looked around and there was no one who could help me. Jimmy and Darryl were sitting at the bar with their backs turned to the window. As I looked through the window I prayed that Jimmy would break from the conversation and look in my direction, but he never even looked.

"How bout that smoke though my nigga," said the short Italian dude in a voice imitating a black street thug. I reached into my inside pocket and gripped my Colt 45. The sound of the bigger guy cocking his pistol made me let go of it and pull out the pack of Newport's instead. I shook one out of the pack and held it out to the short dude who looked like Danny DiVitto in a black suit.

"That's the last time you'll be grabbing that pistol! As a matter of fact, Mario take that fucking thing before he hurts his fucking self," he said as he reached for the cigarette.

A punch hit me across my jaw, and then I was grabbed up again by the bigger guy. He reached into my

CLARK KENT

jacket and took my pistol. He held me against the wall with one hand as he put my pistol in his waist band with the other.

"Mario! What the fuck are you doing huh? That ain't no way to treat our guest for the evening. Put him down and let's go meet his friends inside," the short guy said as he stubbed out his cigarette on the wall next to my head. The big guy lifted me up and straightened out my shirt and jacket.

"Listen, you fucking scumbag pimp bastard. If you so much as blink without my permission I'll kill you, your nigger uncle and the nigger preacher too! Do you understand?" As he said it the bigger guy he looked at me as if he were a demon.

"I get it motherfucka!" I said as I got myself to my feet. I figured my chances were better with Darryl and Jimmy with me. I walked back into the bar and headed to the end of the bar where my uncle and my brother were sitting. I sat next to Jimmy and the two Italians sat next to us.

"Well good evening gentleman. To what do we owe the honor?" Jimmy asked as he sipped his glass of Scotch.

YELLOW CLEVELAND – The Man of Peace

"It seems that this young fella is connected to some missing merchandise sought out by my boss Mr. Sammy Carabotta," the short Italian said as he waved for the bartender. Jimmy looked at me as if he had no idea what the Italian was talking about.

"Do you have something that belongs to these gentleman, nephew?" he asked as the bartender came over and took a round of drink orders.

"No, I have no idea what they are talking about," I said. I looked at my brother who had no idea what was going on, and was looking at me like I had just gotten busted doing something that I had no business doing. The bartender came back with our drinks. As she passed them out she looked very nervous. I wondered if even she knew what was happening.

"Here's to finding the truth and returning what belong to my boss," the short Italian said as he raised his glass. Everyone else at the table picked up their glasses as if to toast to what he was saying. I couldn't believe I was being set up to take the fall for a heist that I wasn't even supposed to be involved in.

"We're going to take a little ride to meet up with Mr. C. If everything goes right we'll bring your nephew right back," the short Italian said as he stood up from the bar.

"I know exactly who your boss is. Tell Sammy that if anything happens to my nephew there will be hell to pay," Jimmy said as he picked up another shot glass. "Like I said I happen to know exactly who your boss is and he knows who I am. So if my nephew is harmed in any way I will personally see to it that none of you lives to see another day on this earth," Jimmy said as he spun around on his stool.

"Well, let's go to talk to your boss and get all of this straightened out!" I said as I downed my drink. I stood up and motioned for the Italians to follow me out of the door. Darryl stood up but Jimmy put a hand up to stop him. Jimmy nodded at me as if to say he was going to take care of this situation. I walked out of the door and left with the Italians, not knowing that I could possibly be dead within the next few hours.

As I walked towards the exit my mind flashed to when Jimmy had told me that everything had gone down as planned thanks to me. I remembered him telling me that my account was already set up. I walked out of the bar and it was clear that the only thing that had been set up was for me to be the scape goat.

YELLOW CLEVELAND – The Man of Peace

The Italians escorted me back to the S.U.V. where a driver was sitting behind the wheel. I was shoved into the back seat and the bigger Italian climbed in beside me. The shorter guy jumped into the front passenger seat and the S.U.V sped off.

Chapter 4

The Set Up

As soon as the truck started rolling my head was slammed into the center console between the front and back seats. The short Italian in the front seat hit me with a stiff elbow to the nose. I collapsed into the back seat only to be punched in the stomach by the bigger Italian guy. I was hit in the head by some sort of sharp object and lost consciousness.

When I woke up I was tied to a chair in the middle of an empty room. The only light was a hanging light with a pyramid lampshade that only lit the room in a small portion below where the light hung. I could hear the sounds of someone else being beaten in a nearby room.

My head was pounding and I felt like I had been in a car accident. My ribs were sore, and it hurt to breath. My entire face felt swollen and I could feel blood running down the side of my face.

The sound of the door opening sent chills down my spine. I could hear heavy footsteps approaching, and the

CLARK KENT

sound of men laughing as if they had just come from a sporting event. In the background I could hear the faint cries of someone who had survived a brutal beating.

"Get this piece of shit to his fucking feet! And take the fucking tape off of his mouth I want to hear what he has to say," said a man with a receding hairline, who was wearing a tuxedo. Another big Italian walked over and cut the rope that I had been tied to the chair with then snatched the duct tape from my mouth. Next he grabbed me by the back of my shirt and lifted me to my feet.

"Look, I don't have time to be fucking around with you about this shit! Do you understand me? I am going to ask you one question and the answer that I get will either give you life, or it will give you death. Do you understand me?"

"However this is an open book test so to speak... I will tell you the first answer that will not be accepted. You will not tell me that you don't know where my diamonds went after they left your possession. With that being said, I ask you, where are my fucking diamonds?" the man with the receding hairline asked as he approached me.

I thought about what Uncle Jimmy had said about there being hell to pay if anything happened to me. I

YELLOW CLEVELAND – The Man of Peace

thought about seeing Diamond with a bullet in her forehead. I knew that the whole heist had been set up by Smooth, and Pretty Tony and I knew that I had been set up to take the fall for it all.

When I didn't answer I was hit in the side of the head with what felt like a 2X4. I fell to my knees only to be yanked up by the back of my shirt again.

"I forgot to tell you that this is a timed test. When I ask a question you only have three seconds to respond. If you do not answer within the three seconds allotted there will be a penalty," the guy with the receding hairline said as he grabbed me by the top of my head.

My mind flashed to a time when Jersey had told me that she didn't like the new Italian guys who Jimmy had been working for. She had said they were evil monsters who fed on violence. She had told me about a pimp who they had fed to a pig because he had snitched on them.

I was brought back from my stupor by a stun gun to my ribs. My body jumped and I was knocked off of my feet. When I landed on the floor I couldn't see. Everything had gone white and I felt numb. I was snatched up again and hit several times in the face and then thrown into the chair again.

CLARK KENT

The door opened and I could hear the sound of someone else being shuffled into the room. I could hear the sound of another chair being unfolded and set out for the person to be seated in.

I thought about the first time that my father had taken me to the gym to box. I knew that if I just held on I could make it through this. I thought back to when I had gotten jumped in Junior High school. I remembered hearing Dawn's soft sweet voice just before I opened my eyes.

As I sat there consumed in thought yet barely even conscious I was awakened by cold water being dumped on me from a bucket. I opened my eyes and my sight was blurry. I could see what looked like someone in a chair across from me. I was seeing double and my ears were ringing.

I squinted my eyes and saw that it was Valerie who was now tied to the chair across from me. I had seen her at the funeral, but we hadn't really been seeing each other lately. Her face was swollen and her clothes were ripped.

"We got your bitch! And you know what she told us after a little bit of constructive questioning? She told us that you gave the diamonds to your friend and fellow piece of shit Mr. Pretty Tony! So before you try to tell us you don't know where our merchandise is, remember that what you say could cost your precious little bitch her life," the Italian said just before he hit her with a mean uppercut to the chin.

Her head snapped back and she began to cry. I looked around and saw that there were at least four other men in the room. Some of them wore shoulder holsters with pistols; the others were dressed like they were in an Italian mafia movie. One of the men walked over and started hitting her over and over like a punching bag. I thought they were going to kill her. I couldn't stand watching them torture her like that. I had to do something to make them stop.

"My cousin set it up! We had nothing to do with it. All I was doing was trying to stay alive," I said as I sat myself upright.

"Where are the diamonds now?" he asked.

"I gave em to the person who my cousin was supposed to take them to. I wasn't even supposed to have anything to do with it. My cousin came to me at the last minute and said he needed my help with a heist he had set up for some Italians. Everything that happened after that was in an attempt to live and get past all of this," I explained as I tried to get my eyes to focus.

"Bring me that asshole from next door," the Italian said looking over his shoulders at two big guys standing in the shadows. The two men left the room and came back dragging a man who looked to be unconscious. The man had a gash in his forehead and was bleeding profusely. He was thrown to the ground in front of me. When he looked up I saw that it was Pretty Tony.

One of the Italians kicked him in his ribs and he collapsed to the floor. The Italian kicked him again this time in the jaw as he tried to get up. His body fell to the floor again, and his eyes seemed to stare into space.

"Is this piece of shit the person you gave my diamond to?" The Italian asked the question looking at me as he stood over Tony's nearly lifeless body. They had beaten him so badly that he was hardly even recognizable.

"I can't even see what he looks like. I don't know who that is," I cried as I looked down at his beaten face. The Italians picked him up and put him in a chair. A bucket of water was dumped on his head and he bobbed his head as if he was trying to wake himself up. Another bucket of water was poured over his head.

YELLOW CLEVELAND – The Man of Peace

"Mr. Pretty Tony you have one chance to save the lives of the three of you. I'm only going to ask one time, if you don't give me the right answer you all die," the Italian with the receding hairline said. "Where are my fucking diamonds?" he yelled as loud as he could as he cocked the hammer of his revolver back. Tony somehow managed to open his eyes.

"There on the way to Tucson to be sold at the Gem and mineral show! There is supposed to be a meeting set up in a hotel called The Hotel Arizona somewhere downtown! Do what you gotta do to me but let them go they had nothing to do with it," Pretty Tony said as he looked around the room.

The Italian pointed his pistol and shot Pretty Tony in the head. Brain matter and blood seemed to splatter everywhere. His body fell to the floor. The Italian walked over and spit on him. He turned around and kicked me in the chest knocking me out of the chair. My head hit the floor and I could feel blood running down my face.

"You are going to Tucson pal and you will do what ever you must do in order to bring me my diamonds. If you don't return my diamonds and or my money within the next twenty four hours, I will kill your little black bitch first, and then I will go to Cleveland and personally

CLARK KENT

fuck your sister before I cut her to pieces. Are we clear Mr. Gaines? You piece of shit," he said as he stood in front of me. I sat there frozen wondering how they knew my name and how they knew about my sister in Cleveland. I didn't even really know where she was, but somehow these guys had already found out about her.

I looked at Pretty Tony's body lying on the ground with a big portion of the top of his head blown off. It looked like something you'd see in a horror movie.

"I don't think this nigger can hear. Benny I told you not to fuck him up too bad, look at this fucking gumba! Can you hear me you piece of shit thief?" he yelled into my ear.

"Yes! I got it, I hear you," I cried out. Out of nowhere a hard object hit me in the back of my head. My sight went white again and the ringing in my ears got so loud it became deafening. I fell to the floor as I was hit several more times in the face and head. One of the Italians started kicking me in my ribs over and over.

"Enough! Clean this fucking piece of shit up and drop him back off where you found him," the Italian said as he snatched up Valerie by the hair. "I'm going to go spend some time with his little nigger bitch," he said as he pushed her towards the door. Another bucket of

YELLOW CLEVELAND – The Man of Peace

water was poured over my head and one of the Italians lifted me to my feet and handed me a towel to wipe my face with.

An hour later I was thrown out of the S.U.V. in front of The District bar in Newport Beach. It was nearly midnight and the bar was crowded. I walked in and it seemed like everybody stopped talking and turned to look at me. I had blood running down my face and one of my eyes was swollen shut. My ribs hurt so bad that I could barely even breathe. I fell to the floor and passed out.

Chapter 5

The Light in the Darkness

At first I couldn't tell if I was dreaming or awake. There was nothing. All I saw was white. I sat up and tried to focus my eyes but there was nothing to focus on. There were no walls, no ceiling, and no sound. I closed my eyes and when I opened them again I was in some kind of morgue.

I walked to the first stretcher and lifted the cover off of the body. It was my sister. She looked like she had been tortured to death. I dropped the cover and stumbled back. I walked over to the next stretcher and lifted the cover only to see my brother Darryl with his throat slashed. My head started to spin, but I needed to see who the other bodies were.

I walked to the next stretcher and lifted the blanket. It was Dawn. Her face looked normal but her entire abdomen was covered with blood. I lifted the cover to see her body and was stricken with fear. She had been cut from her vagina to her breasts. I couldn't take it anymore I needed to get away from all of the bodies.

CLARK KENT

I started to walk away and as I did everything went dark. I tried to scream but there was no sound. When I turned around I could see light in the distance. My mind told me that the people I loved were back there somewhere in the light. I tried to walk back to it but the more I walked the further the light seemed to get. I tried to run but it felt like I was running in place. I needed to get back to them. My heart seemed to be pounding so hard that I felt like my chest was going to explode.

Then I started to hear voices. The light was gone and everything was dark. I could hear someone saying that it didn't look like I was going to make it. I couldn't feel anything, I couldn't open my eyes but I knew I was in some sort of hospital room.

I could hear the sounds of different medical machines. One sounded like it was breathing and I could also hear what sounded like a heart monitor. I heard a voice that I didn't recognize asking someone about what had happened to me. I could tell from the tone of the voice that it had to be a policeman or detective. Then I heard my brother, Darryl's voice telling the officer that the last time he had seen me was when I went to smoke a cigarette.

YELLOW CLEVELAND – The Man of Peace

Hearing Darryl's voice told me that I had to have been dreaming when I saw him dead. It also told me that both Dawn and my sister could still be alive. I heard Jimmy saying that he would do everything he could to find out who had done this to me. I felt angry knowing that he knew exactly who had done this to me.

The voices faded and I found myself back in Vegas with a room full of white women. I was lying in the bed in the center of the room. They were laughing at me and saying that I had done this to myself. The women were all naked and dancing around the bed.

"All you had to do is stay with us and none of this would have ever happened," one of the women said as she sat a tray of white powder beside me. Everything went dark again and then I found myself back in Cleveland at my old house.

My parents were upset because I had quit school. My father was pacing back and forth with a black garbage bag in his hand.

"This shit is going to ruin your life boy! If you think you can just sell drugs and chase women for the rest of your life you're dead wrong," he yelled just before everything went dark again.

CLARK KENT

This time it stayed dark and quiet. I couldn't hear a sound. I could feel myself thinking, but I couldn't feel my body. I thought of what Pretty Tony had said before he was killed. I remembered him saying that the diamonds were on their way to Tucson to be sold at the Gem and Mineral show.

I felt warmth and I began to feel a tingle in my toes. I forced my eyes open and saw Darryl asleep in a chair by my bed. I was in a hospital. I had an oxygen mask over my mouth and I was hooked up to an I.V. machine. Monitors at the foot of the bed were recording my vital signs.

My head was bandaged and my entire body ached. I tried to move but I had been strapped to the bed. Darryl looked up and saw me awake and called for the nurse. A few seconds later the hospital room was filled with doctors and nurses. A doctor shined a light in my eyes and started asking me questions but I couldn't answer because of the oxygen mask. The doctor started giving orders to the other doctors and nurses and everybody scrambled.

The doctor removed the oxygen mask from my face, and began to unbuckle me from the bed. Even without the restraints I still couldn't move. My face still felt swollen and every movement sent pain racing through my body.

"Mr. Gaines you have lost a lot of blood, and you have some broken ribs as well as a broken nose. Your head was busted in three places, and to be honest I am pretty sure you will have some post traumatic stress. Do you know who did this to you?" the doctor asked as he stood over me looking at my charts.

I didn't speak. I lay there wondering how I was going to get the diamonds back to the Italians before they had a chance to kill Valerie and my sister. I remembered seeing my sister dead in my dream, and I tried to sit myself up. As soon as I moved I was thrown back down on the bed by a severe pain in my abdomen.

A man dressed in a shirt and tie walked into the room carrying a cell phone in a Ziploc bag. He placed the bag on the table next to me and sat at the foot of the bed.

"Sir my name is Detective Johnson of the Newport Beach police department. I'm here to try to help you figure out who did this to you. Your boss left you this phone and said he would be in touch. We checked it out and were not able to find any useful information in it. Do you remember what happened?" he asked as he opened a pocket sized notebook.

"I don't remember... The last thing I remember was some guy asking me for a cigarette," I told him.

"Do you remember what he looked like? Did you know him from somewhere?" he asked.

"I can't remember. I didn't get a good look at his face," I said.

"That's interesting because there was a witness who saw you talking to two men outside of the bar," he replied. I looked at him but didn't speak again. He asked a few more questions and then stood up and handed me a business card with his phone number on it. "If you start to remember something please be sure to call me," he said as he walked out of the room.

Darryl had been standing in the hallway outside of the room and he came in when the detective left. At first he just stood there looking at me. He shook his head and a tear rolled down his cheek.

"Bro we gotta get you home. I don't know how you got yourself mixed up in all of this foolishness, but you can't stay here," he said as he came and sat beside me.

"They have a friend of mine and if we don't get those diamonds back to them they are going to kill her... They also said they were going to go to Cleveland and kill Amy if I didn't get the diamonds back," I said in a low voice.

"Who are they?" he asked.

"The Italian mafia," I told him.

"How in the hell do they know about Amy?" he asked.

"I have no idea. They killed a friend of mine who told them that the diamonds were being taken to Tucson to be sold at the Gem and Mineral show. How long have I been here?" I asked.

"Two days," he replied. I thought about Amy and Valerie. I remembered the Italian saying that I had twenty four hours to get the diamonds back. I realized that it had now been forty-eight hours since they threw me out of the S.U.V.

"Fuck! We gotta get on the horn to Cleveland and get Amy somewhere safe while we figure out what to do," I said to him as I tried once again to sit myself upright. The pain hit me again but I couldn't let it get the best of me this time. I grunted and pulled myself into a sitting position. Just as I got myself up the cell phone inside of the Ziploc started ringing. Darryl grabbed the bag and handed me the phone.

"Well, it looks like my little errand boy is alive after all. I knew you could do it," a voice on the other end of the phone said when I answered it. "In view of your current situation I decided to give you more time. You now have forty-eight hours to get off of your ass and get me my diamonds. And if you tell the police anything I'm going to kill my new houseguest. Kapish?" It was the man whose voice I recognized as the guy with the receding hairline. Before I could answer the phone went dead.

"What did they say?" Darryl asked.

"They said we have forty-eight hours," I told him. I sat there wondering what they had already done to Valerie and wondering how to find the diamonds. Darryl got on his phone and started talking to someone about getting Amy out of harms way. When he left the room I dialed Jimmy's number. When he didn't answer I realized that he wouldn't recognize the number and therefore would not answer so I left a message.

An hour later Jimmy showed up at the hospital. I told him about what had happened and he told me not to worry about the Italians. He said he had already sent someone to get the diamonds. He also said that when this was all over he wanted me and Valerie to disappear for a while.

Jimmy motioned for Darryl to give us a moment to talk. When Darryl closed the door Jimmy sat down next to me. When he sat down he looked like he was the cat who swallowed the canary.

"I already got the diamonds back. I'm going to make the drop and get Candy out of there and then we are going to get some revenge. While you were there did you see if they had Tony?" he asked.

"I saw them kill him right in front of me. His fuckin brains splattered all over me," I said as I tried to lay myself back down.

"Fuck! Don't worry nephew I got boys too. Everything that they did to y' all, is coming back ten fold on those sons of bitches. I gotta get you out of here right now though. Darryl! Get me a wheel chair," he yelled as he stood up and started pacing the room.

Darryl came back with a wheelchair and Jimmy helped me get into it. A nurse came into the room and asked what was going on and Jimmy told her that we were going to the cafeteria.

CLARK KENT

Another nurse who Jimmy must've paid came in after the first nurse was gone and removed the I.V. needles from my arm and handed Jimmy a bag with bottles of pills. She looked into the hallway and made sure no one was coming and motioned for us to leave. Jimmy pushed the wheelchair while Darryl grabbed my belongings and we left the Hoag Hospital in the early hours of the morning.

Chapter 6
Ready Set Go

As soon as we were in the car the cell phone that was left by my so called "boss" started ringing. I answered after a few rings and just as I figured, it was the man with the receding hairline.

"Ready! Set! Go! The clock is ticking. I will call you in forty-eight hours with instructions. Don't miss my call or I will cut little Miss Valerie here to pieces. Enjoy your ride," he said. The phone went dead and I turned off the phone.

"We got a tail fellas, sit back I'll show you how to fix this," Uncle Jimmy said as he swerved through traffic switching lanes and passing cars. I looked out of the back window and saw the car that was following us was doing the same. As if in a movie Jimmy spun the steering wheel and made the fastest left turn imaginable. He drove through an alley and turned left onto 32nd street. After snaking through a couple of side streets we tuned onto Balboa and blended into traffic.

CLARK KENT

As a professional driver Uncle Jimmy never missed an opportunity to show off his skills. He could get out of any kind of situation. Jimmy decided to take us to his rental property on 24th street off of Balboa right around the corner from The District bar.

It was a two story house near the beach that he usually rented out to tourist for beach getaways. Jimmy had made a few calls and already had people meeting us there.

When we pulled into the driveway of the house the garage door opened and we pulled in next to another black Lincoln town car. Once we were in, the garage door closed and we got out and went into the house.

We walked up to the second floor and into a room set up like a bar. A 60 inch T.V. took up a good portion of the wall at the far end of the room. An oak bar stretched the length of another wall with bar stools lined up against it. On the opposite side of the room there was a set of sliding doors leading to a balcony. Jimmy opened the sliding doors and we walked onto the balcony.

A group of men who I didn't recognize were sitting on lounge chairs with drinks in their hands. They made a toast, downed the drinks and then stood up to greet us.

YELLOW CLEVELAND – The Man of Peace

"Damn boss you must be getting old it took you forever to get here. We were beginning to wonder if you had meant for us to pick you up," one of the men said as he reached out and shook Jimmy's hand laughing.

"I was testing you. I got here last on purpose. I know you aint up in here drinkin on the job," Jimmy said as he pulled him in for a hug. Jimmy introduced us to the men who turned out to be a hit squad that Jimmy had pulled together. One of the men went inside and brought out glasses and we all took shots of tequila then Jimmy filled them in on what was going on.

"It seems that one of my former clients has decided to play by old rules. He thinks because he is Italian that he is the fuckin Godfather or somebody. His ass is about to find out that these are my stompin grounds," he said as he poured us all another shot.

The pain in my ribs was starting to come back so I took a couple of the pills that the nurse had given me. As I sat there, I was getting madder by the minute. Not only had they worked me and Valerie over, I had been forced to watch a man who was like a mentor to me get his head blown off. I wanted them all dead

"Ace I don't want you to move a muscle on this. I'll take it from here. Sam I want to send a message to our

CLARK KENT

friend that I have the diamonds and I want a meet. Will I want you to find out where they are keeping Candy. Also Sam, reach out to T and B. Tell them I want them with us every step of the way on this one. Darryl I want you to stay here and make sure your brother stays low key for a couple days until I get this shit taken care of." Jimmy walked back inside to the bar and picked up a remote control and turned on the T.V. As much as I wanted to get my own revenge I was in no shape to argue.

I saw Jimmy put a black velvet bag into a box and hide the box behind the bar. He looked out to the patio to make sure no one had seen him stash the box. He came back to the patio with a drink in his hand as if he had only gone to the bar to get a drink. I figured that it had to be the diamonds in the box he had stashed. I decided that when the time was right I was going to switch some of the diamonds with fake ones and keep some of the diamonds for myself.

The crew got up to leave and Jimmy walked them out. I stayed on the balcony letting the cool ocean breeze sooth my swollen face. Darryl came out and stood by the banister looking at the view.

YELLOW CLEVELAND – The Man of Peace

"Bro I'm glad you made it out of all that alive. I prayed for you bro, but I didn't know what the hell was going on," Darryl said as he lit a cigarette.

"You let them walk out of there with me bro. Shit I'm sure you didn't think they were friends of mine," I said as I struggled to get myself up and on my feet.

"You're right; I did let them walk out of there with you. I really didn't know what in the hell was going on. I figured Jimmy knew more about what was going on than I did, and he told me to let you go with them. What was I supposed to do? I'm not like you anymore bro! I don't go runnin the damn streets lookin for trouble anymore! I don't go getting myself into stupid situations anymore either bro," Darryl said.

"Whatever nigga! I do what I gotta do to survive and get this money! You taught me that. Just because you found Jesus don't make you a saint bro," I told him as I walked over to the banister.

"Look bro the bottom line is that it was because of the grace of God that you're still alive. You're right I didn't jump up and get myself wrapped up in something I wasn't involved in. I didn't come out here for that. But everything that has happened is proof that you need to roll back to Cleveland with me," Darryl said.

CLARK KENT

"I got money out here in these streets. I can't just up and leave. People depend on me. That shit that happened don't normally happen to me. I got people out here. I got killers on my squad. Trust me bro that shit is getting handled. I'm good out here," I told him.

"At least take a break and come see the family bro," Darryl said. I thought about it for a second then told him that if he could stay out here long enough for my face to heal up then I would consider going for a visit. In the meantime I decided that we needed some company so I called two of my home girls and asked if they would bring me some weed and come hang with us for a while. While I was on the phone Jimmy came back in and tossed a set of keys to Darryl.

"I don't want him going to his apartment or anywhere else that he usually goes. I'm leaving one of the cars in the garage, but I would prefer that you two don't go too far from here. I have a few things to do but if you fellas need anything call me," he said as he walked out of the door.

An hour later, Monique, and her friend Brandy showed up. Monique was very pretty. She was black and Latino, Brandy was a pretty Native American girl. I had met Monique at Venice Beach. She was just walking into

YELLOW CLEVELAND – The Man of Peace

a medical marijuana shop as I was on my way out. When our eyes met I turned around and decided that I needed to do a little more shopping.

"Oh my God baby what happened to you?" Brandy asked when she walked into the room. The concern in her eyes gave her an irresistible look. It was as if she could feel my pain.

"You should see the other guy baby," I said as I forced myself up and onto my feet. I guess she was able to tell how much it was hurting me to move because she dropped her purse and ran to my side.

"Daddy, please! Sit your handsome self down; you look like you were hit by a train. Mama's here now. You just sit back and rest," she said as she grabbed my face and kissed me on my swollen eye. I could tell from the concern in her voice that I looked even worse than I felt, which was hard to imagine because I felt like I had been hit by two trains. "You remember Brandy don't you?" she asked. I remembered Brandy for sure but I wasn't about to tell her why.

Brandy and I had run into each other in Riverside and went out for drinks. By the end of the night we had a secret that neither of us wanted Monique to know. In

CLARK KENT

fact we had to be careful because we had found out that we were very sexually compatible.

"Ladies, this is my older brother Darryl. He's here on vacation so to speak. Bro, these two beautiful young ladies are very dear friends of mine," I said. Brandy was wearing Daisy Duke Shorts and a bikini top. Her voluptuous breast looked like they were going to escape if she breathed too hard. Monique was wearing a sexy sundress with her hair in a ponytail.

Monique pulled out a small jar from her purse with some of the prettiest weed I had ever seen. When she opened the jar the weed was so strong that it permeated the room. She dumped it onto the bar and started breaking it up to roll a blunt.

"Can I get you ladies a drink?" I asked as I tried once again to get myself to my feet.

"No! If anything I should be asking you if you want a drink," Brandy said. She stood up and walked around to the other side of the bar. I couldn't help watching her. She seemed to float as she walked. I thought about how sexy she was naked wearing only her 6 inch heels. This was the first time I had seen them both since Brandy and I had enjoyed an evening at my apartment.

YELLOW CLEVELAND – The Man of Peace

"Are you married Darryl?" Monique asked as if she was trying to stop me from staring at Brandy.

"No, I was but it didn't work out," he said.

"Brandy is single. You should get to know her. I think she could use a man like you in her life," Monique said as she licked the blunt and finished rolling it. Brandy didn't skip a beat.

"Uh, hello! How do you know I need a man girl? For all you know I could have a man and have just decided not to tell you about him," Brandy said as she sat four glasses on the bar.

"Girl I would know. If I remember correctly you haven't had a man since you broke up with Robert," Monique said as she lit the blunt.

"Girl you just don't know! I may not have been in a relationship since then but I have had a man in the sheets with me once or twice since then," Brandy said laughing as she poured us all shots of Tequila. As she said it she kind of winked in my direction.

"I have an idea. After we have a few drinks and get our smoke on, let's go around the corner and get something to eat. I'm starving," I said in an attempt to change the subject.

CLARK KENT

"I feel you bro I could go for some seafood right about now," Darryl said. Monique came over and handed me the blunt. As soon as I inhaled I broke out into a painful coughing fit. It was like I was being hit with a bat. I handed the blunt back to her and clutched my ribs. Darryl got up and handed me the bag of pills from the hospital.

"It's probably not such a good idea for you to be coughing with broken ribs Bro," he said. Monique tried to hand him the blunt but he refused. Both girls looked at him like he was an alien or something.

"You're not going to smoke with us Darryl?" Monique asked as she passed the blunt to Brandy.

"No, I stopped smoking weed years ago baby," he told her.

"Why?" Brandy asked as she took a long pull from the blunt.

"It's a long story, but if it will make you more comfortable I will hit it a few times for old time sake."

As we smoked the rest of the blunt Darryl and Brandy sat at the bar getting to know each other. Monique got up and poured another round of shots and came to sit by me.

YELLOW CLEVELAND – The Man of Peace

"Baby I have really been missing you," she said as she raised her glass. I thought about the toast that the Italians made at the District and a chill went through my body.

"I been missing you too baby," I said as I downed my drink to wash down the pain pills.

"I'm not going anywhere Daddy. I need to spend some time with you. After we go out to eat I want to come back here and help you get some rest," she said. We finished our drinks and got up to leave.

Chapter 7
Footprints

We walked out of the house and decided to go towards the beach, which was literally a stones throw away from the house. At the corner of the street there was a bicycle rental shop.

We decided to rent two of the double seat pedal cars and cruise the beach for a while. Monique decided to do the pedaling because of the pain I was in. I sat in the passenger side and watched as people we rode past people on the boardwalk.

It was just after 7:00 in the evening, and the sun was starting to set. The light blue skies with hints of thin clouds in the distance had started to give way to yellow clouds on a pink horizon.

We rode at a nice slow pace enjoying the scenery I noticed that Monique had that far away look in her eyes as if she had something on her mind. At first I didn't say anything, but after awhile the silence began to feel awkward.

CLARK KENT

"What's on your mind baby?" I asked.

"What makes you think there is something on my mind?" she replied by asking.

"Well for starters you haven't said anything since we started riding. Is everything okay?" I asked. She looked away as her eyes began to tear up. She pulled the bike to the side of the trail and stopped.

"I do have something I need to talk to you about, but I wanted to wait until we were alone," she said as she wiped a tear from her cheek. We got out of the pedal car and walked across the sand to the beach. The sand glittered in the water as the waves washed back out to sea. The cold water soothed my feet as I stood looking at the sunset. I wondered what it was that she needed to talk to me about, but I didn't want to pry.

Everything was usually all business with us. There was no real commitment between us other than the fact that we occasionally had really good sex. We had told each other that we would always keep our relationship as more of a friendship than anything, so I wondered why she suddenly felt like there was something she needed to say to me.

I wondered if it had anything to do with what had happened to me. I began to think she was going soft on me or something. I looked at her but still didn't force the conversation.

The last rays of the sun danced across her face as the wind blew through her hair. She was definitely beautiful. I grabbed her hand and started to walk towards the pier. The sound of the waves crashing on the beach was like therapy. It was almost hard to believe that just two days ago I had gone through the worst day of my life.

When we got to the pier she stopped and looked me in my eyes. Her eyes told me that whatever she had on her mind was hurting her. I hugged her tightly and kissed her cheek. I wanted her to know that I was there for her just as she had been there for me.

"I'm pregnant," she said in a sob as she pulled away from me. "I know what you're thinking, and I'm not saying that it's yours. To tell the truth I wish it was, but I can't say that I know for sure it is," she told me as she began to cry.

"Wow I didn't see that coming. What do you want to do?" I asked

"I'm keeping it... I want it. More than anything I wish I could say that it's yours but you know I was with still with my ex when we first started messing around. When

CLARK KENT

I told him, he told me to get an abortion. I didn't want to because I knew it was possible that it wasn't his. I really want it to be yours, but I really don't know," she said with tears rolling down her cheek.

I had never thought about having a kid before. I had always been careful not to get anybody pregnant, but as I stood there looking at the water I couldn't help but to wonder what it would be like to be a father.

I thought back to the last time we had made love. That night we had gone four rounds and the pack of condoms only had three condoms in it. We were drunk. I remembered her waking up in the morning and leaving in a hurry.

That was when I found out that she had a man. It had been at least three months since then. At the time I didn't think anything of it. She had been coming to me for weed at least twice a week since then and she never even mentioned it.

"Baby I really don't know what to say other than the fact that I'm here for you. I can't let you go through this alone. Shit, I kind of wish it was mines now that I think of it," I told her as I pulled her close to me. As I said it I wondered if I was making a mistake. She was married

YELLOW CLEVELAND – The Man of Peace

and if she wanted to stay with her husband I definitely didn't want to get in their way.

"You don't have to do that. I don't want you to have to wonder if it's someone else's baby. I don't want this to tear us apart either," she said as she turned and looked at the water.

"I'm here for you! Let's just take it one day at a time. Right now I want you to stop worrying. I want you to know that what ever you decide to do I will have your back!" I told her.

"Do you really mean that?" she asked as she looked up at me through teary eyes.

"Yes! That's my promise to you," I said as I wiped the tears from her cheek. "Now quit getting all soft on me and let's go enjoy our evening. I guess you could say that we have some celebrating to do,"

"Ace you have no idea how much this means to me. I didn't expect you to react this way. I can't thank you enough. I love you Ace," she said we started walking back to the pedal cars. I didn't answer her. I really didn't know what to say. On one hand I was kind of happy, on the other hand I wondered if I really was ready for a family.

CLARK KENT

I looked back at the two sets of footprints we were leaving in the sand and kind of giggled to myself. In the words of Smooth I was about to become a square if I wasn't careful, but at the time it felt like the right thing to do. She was going to have a baby and never know for sure if it was mine or not.

When we got back to the pedal cars Darryl was talking to Brandy about how Jesus died for her sins. As we approached I could hear him telling her that all she had to do was ask for forgiveness. When he saw us coming he smiled and stood up.

"Big bro, are you ready to go get something to eat or what?" I asked as I brushed the sand off of my feet and put my sandals back on.

"I thought we were going to have to go without you two love birds," he replied. We took the pedal cars back to the rental place and headed for The Crab Cooker, a restaurant on the other side of Balboa. While we were walking my phone started ringing. I looked at the caller I.D. and saw that it was Uncle Jimmy. I decided not to answer, I figured if it was important enough he would just come to the house.

After we ate we walked back to the house. The pain in my ribs had come back with a vengeance. All I could

YELLOW CLEVELAND – The Man of Peace

think about was getting back to those pills. I had almost forgotten about my swollen face but now my head was pounding.

"Are you okay baby?" Monique asked as we turned onto 24th and headed for the house.

"I think I over did it. My whole body is hurting," I told her.

"I'll make you a nice hot bath and get you together baby," she said as we walked up to the house. Right away I noticed three of Jimmy's cars parked in front of the house. I remembered thinking that if it had been important enough that he would have come to the house. Well from the looks of things it had been important.

When we walked in Sam stood up with his gun in his hand. When he saw that it was us he went to the balcony and motioned for Jimmy. Jimmy came in with a drink in his hand. There was blood on his shirt and pants and he looked very upset. I walked over to him and he motioned for me to come to the porch.

"We got her, but they messed her up really bad. She's at the hospital. I left Will there to watch over her. Ace you're going to have to get out of town for awhile. This thing is far from over they'll be looking for you," he

CLARK KENT

said as he downed his drink. It had gotten dark. The full moon was high in the sky.

"How bad is she?" I asked.

"She looks a lot worse than you did. I know you probably want to see her but I want you to stay away for at least a couple of weeks until things die down. When everything blows over I'll bring her to you. In the meantime I want you to post up here until we can get you and Darryl on the road."

"I don't think I really want to go back to Cleveland right now, I got things here I need to take care of first," I told him.

"Anything that needs to be taken care of here I will personally take care of for you, but I need you to go with Darryl. It's about to get ugly right now and I prefer that you not be here when it does," he said. I stood looking over the balcony. I thought about the diamonds that were stashed in the box behind the bar. I needed to get some fake stones for the switch. This was going to be my payback for Jimmy letting me take the fall for the heist. The pain was getting worse by the minute. As much as I didn't want to, I knew that I really had no choice. I was headed back to Cleveland.

YELLOW CLEVELAND – The Man of Peace

I had Monique take me to an arts and crafts store. I told her that I wanted to buy some paints, and new brushes to give to my father when I got to Cleveland. While we were there I also bought a bag of fake diamonds to make the switch.

As we rode back to the beach house I thought about the fact that if Jimmy were to get caught passing off fake diamonds he would possibly be killed. Then I thought about how he had let the Italians take me out of the bar. An eye for an eye I told myself. The whole situation was bad, but I wasn't going to be leaving empty handed.

Chapter 8
Que Sera Sera

After Jimmy and his crew left I was ready to take a long hot bath to try to ease the pain. I told Monique that I was going to Cleveland for a few weeks to visit my family. I told her I needed to get rid of a couple of pounds of weed before I left and she told me she would make a few calls and get rid of it for me.

That night I really couldn't sleep. I couldn't stop thinking about Cleveland. I hadn't been home in years. I thought about my sister who I had found out was in Georgia visiting some of our cousins. Evidently the Italians had received some bad info. I felt better knowing that she was safe.

I thought about what it was going to be like seeing my parents again. I hadn't seen them since I had gotten thrown out for dropping out of school. Since then it was very rare that I had even been able to get in touch with them.

CLARK KENT

Then I thought about the old gang and wondered what the fellas had been up to, or if they were even still around. I guess it really wasn't such a bad idea to go back home for awhile. I definitely had enough money. All I had been doing was hustling and stacking money since I had gotten to Cali. I was also going to have some diamonds that I would need to sell when I got to Cleveland.

After about two hours of tossing and turning I finally decided to get up and go sit on the balcony. When I opened the door to the balcony Darryl was sitting in one of the chairs smoking a cigarette.

"What up bro?" I asked as I sat in the chair next to him.

"Not much just looking at the stars thinking. What's up with you?" He asked.

"I couldn't really sleep," I replied.

"So I hear that all of this craziness has kind of made you have to roll with me back to the Land. I guess somehow my plan to get you to come back with me ended up working out after all."

"I guess so, although I really wasn't ready yet," I said as I lit a cigarette.

YELLOW CLEVELAND – The Man of Peace

"A lot has changed since you left. Not to mention the fact that Mama and Pops are going to be seriously happy to finally see you," he said.

"I miss them too it's just going to be a little weird seeing them now that I'm grown and all. It wasn't pretty last time we sat down for a chat," I told him.

"Water under the bridge little brother. God forgives and so should you. By the way when was the last time you went to church?" he asked.

"Actually it hasn't really been too long ago. I went with my home girl right after I got back from Vegas," I replied.

"Well, I have to admit I didn't expect to hear that," he said as he stubbed out his cigarette.

"Honestly that was the first time I had stepped into a church since we were kids," I told him.

"We'll get you together bro don't forget I was doing the same things if not worse than you are before I turned my life over to Christ. You need to be born again. You have to repent and ask for forgiveness. Someone once told me that God gives and forgives, man gets and forgets," he said.

CLARK KENT

"You do understand that this is just a visit right?" I asked.

"I hear you bro," he replied.

"I'm going to pour myself a night cap. Do you need anything?" I asked

"I'm good, but if you're going to sit out here for a little bit I'll get it for you," he replied.

"Well while you're at it could you grab those pain pills for me?" I asked

"Yeah, but you know you shouldn't be drinking with those," he said as he got up and went inside. I thought back to one of the times that we got into trouble when we were kids. I was about six and he was about thirteen years old. Someone had written an X on the wall with a blue crayon.

My father saw the crayon writing on the wall and he flipped. He yelled so loud that it seemed like the whole house shook. He called us all into the room and had us all line up.

"Who in the fuck had the audacity to write on my walls!" he yelled. "Which one of you thinks they have the right to write on the walls of the house that I pay for?" he asked. I looked at my sister Amy who looked like she

YELLOW CLEVELAND – The Man of Peace

was about to wet herself and I knew she didn't deserve to get the whooping that was sure to come to the one of us who drew the X.

I looked at my brother Aaron who looked like he was about to cuss Pops out for having the "audacity" to interrupt him from studying for an algebra test, and I knew it would be a bad idea to let him take the rap for it.

Then my eyes landed on Darryl, my big step brother. If he took the blame for writing on the wall there really wouldn't be any real repercussions. He wouldn't even get a whooping. I knew that because he only came on the weekends and because his mother would give Pops hell if she found out he hit her son, he was going to take the rap.

Sure enough as soon as Pops took off his belt Darryl started crying. He pled and cried and told Pops he was sorry for writing on the wall. I watched the whole thing play out. Darryl had to stay inside for the rest of the day, and he was going to be in serious trouble when his mother came to pick him up.

In reality the X was where my imaginary treasure was hidden. I had been pretending to be a pirate with a treasure map. The blue crayon was in my pocket. I had

CLARK KENT

been spared because my big brother had taken the heat for me.

Once again my big brother had come to the rescue. He was here to get me out of a mess that I was in, but this time it wasn't my fault. All I had done was decide to go to Vegas in memory of my girl Jersey. Running into Smooth was a matter of sheer coincidence.

Now the whole thing had backfired and turned into world war three. I knew that in reality if I stayed in California that I would eventually run into the Italians again. I knew that Jimmy hadn't really intended on giving the diamonds back and that was going to make matters even worse.

Darryl came back out with the bottle of pills and handed it to me. I poured two of the pills into my hand and put them into my mouth. I was sort of getting used to the pain but I still needed the pills.

"What happened to that night cap bro?" I asked.

"Monique is getting it together for you. I guess everybody is having trouble sleeping. Her and Brandy are about to come hang out with us," he said as he sat down next to me.

YELLOW CLEVELAND – The Man of Peace

"So what's up bro? It looks like you and Brandy have been hanging kind of tough," I said. Before he could answer the sliding door opened and the girls came out to join us. Monique had on my T-shirt and not much else from the looks of it. She handed me my drink and sat down with me. Brandy lit a blunt and sat next to Darryl.

A refreshing breeze blew across the patio bringing with it the smell of the ocean. The palm trees swayed back and forth as if they were dancing to the song that the wind was singing. I sat there looking at Monique thinking about the baby she was having. I wondered if it was going to be a boy.

"You know I feel bad for all of you. I see how the lifestyles you all choose to lead can bring about some pretty compromising situations. When I was up there at the funeral it made me sad to see how easily it could have been one of you in those caskets. I'm not trying to lecture you all but, that's what I have been sitting out here thinking about. Bro we're getting on the road in the morning. And ladies I suggest that you all get into some classes and educate yourselves while you're still young enough to position yourself in the game of life." As Darryl said it, it was like the winds stopped.

CLARK KENT

We sat there absorbing the point he was making. I thought about seeing Smooth and Diamond in that hotel room dead. I thought about when I thought I had seen Dawn in Vegas. I wondered what my life would've been like if I hadn't let my teenage mentality cause me to break up with Dawn. I would probably be some dude with a 9 to 5 job.

I looked at Monique and thought about her situation. Pregnant by either me or her husband but unable to really even know. I thought about the fact that I needed to get my G.E.D. and get into a college. As much fun as the street life in L.A. was it always ended too early for people.

It's like no matter what you'll always be chasing something. As we sat looking at the night sky filled with stars, it seemed like the universe had opened up and I could make the right move and get out of the game.

"You better keep in touch with me while you're out there getting things together!" Monique said as she passed me the blunt.

"Baby you know I'll be in touch. I meant what I said," I told her as inhaled a thick cloud of smoke from the blunt. I closed my eyes and tried to clear my mind as I exhaled the smoke through my nose. The smoke made me look like a fire breathing dragon. I started coughing so hard that it caused my ribs to hurt again.

Suddenly, calmness came over me. I could hear the sound of the waves splashing onto the beach. My mind was clear for the moment. I had decided that I was going to go with the flow and see how everything turned out. This was God's plan not mine.

Monique stood up and grabbed my hand. She gave me a seductive look and led me towards the Sliding doors. As she walked I looked at the shape of her body in my T-shirt. She had curvy hips and sexy legs. I followed her to the bedroom and commenced to getting a proper send off.

Chapter 9
Easy Like Sunday Morning

The next morning I woke up to the smell of breakfast cooking. The smell of the bacon gave me a flashback. As I lay there I felt the presence of my family back when we were kids. I imagined that I was 10 years old again. I pictured my dad in the living room smoking a joint listening to the Commodores or Otis Redding.

My mother was in the kitchen cooking breakfast. It was the family ritual to get up early and eat breakfast before church on Sunday mornings I remembered how Darryl always threw his pillow at me. Aaron would be on his bed looking at us like he thought we had lost our minds. The sound of the bedroom door opening jolted me from my daydream.

"I made you breakfast," Monique said as she came in carrying a plate of scrambled eggs, bacon, toast, and hash browns. She was smiling so wide that she was glowing. She sat the plate on the table next to me and sat down beside me.

CLARK KENT

"You know, last night was kind of different. We never really bonded like that before," she said as she kissed my forehead. Her eyes had a look of happiness in them.

"I'm really glad we had a chance to kick it and discuss our situation. I meant what I said. I'm here for you," I said as I sat up to eat my breakfast. She had done an excellent job; it had been a long time since I had last had a home cooked breakfast. After breakfast Monique took a shower and got herself dressed for the day.

She came out of the bathroom an hour later looking like an angel. She had on a white sun dress and white heels carrying a white purse. Her hair hung down around her shoulders.

I stared at her as she walked out to me on the patio. She walked with grace. Her hips swayed perfectly as she glided across the room. Things were definitely not finished between us. I told myself that as soon as everything cleared up I was coming back for her. She had taken my heart over the last twenty four hours.

Before now I hadn't even realized that we had been getting so close. Now it felt like I was leaving her and I knew I would definitely miss her. On top of that she was

YELLOW CLEVELAND – The Man of Peace

pregnant with the baby. She walked over and sat next to me.

"Well baby have a safe trip, and make sure you call me every night before you go to sleep. I have some things to take care of right quick plus I need to take care of that business for you before you ride out," she said as she kissed me on the cheek.

"Call me as soon as you got the money so we can roll out. I want to be on the road by 5:00 this evening," I said as she got up to leave. Brandy came out wearing a red sundress and heels. She too looked beautiful. We walked them out to their car and waved them off.

Darryl called and had Uncle Jimmy drop off his van and my things from the apartment. I had Darryl drive me to a craft store but I didn't tell him why. I bought some art supplies to give to my Pops and a bag of fake diamonds to make the switch before Jimmy got back. I figured that by the time Jimmy or anybody else found out that not all of the diamonds were real I would be long gone.

I couldn't believe it but I had decided to give up the streets of California to go back and start over. I had made it. This was my chance to go home and figure out

CLARK KENT

what I wanted to do with my life. The past five years had been a non stop chain of events.

Every decision had a cause and effect on how my life had turned out. I was smart enough to understand that I hadn't made the best choices in life. I also knew that I couldn't spend the rest of my life running the streets.

I went back out to the patio to absorb the ocean breeze one last time before we hit the road. Half an hour later Jimmy called. He said they had the van packed and that they were on there way to drop it off. I told Darryl and he asked me to pray with him.

"Dear Heavenly father," he said when we bowed our heads. "You have given me the ways and means for this trip to be a successful intervention for my little brother. I thank you for sending angels to watch over us, and we pray that you can deliver us back to Cleveland safe. Heavenly father we ask that you reach out to my brother and show him a better way. We know that you died on the cross for our sins and we ask that our sins can be forgiven. In Jesus name we pray. Amen," he said as he held on to my hands. He pulled me in for a hug.

After we prayed I decided it was time to switch the diamonds. I went to the bar and found the box that Jimmy had stashed the diamonds in. I opened the box

YELLOW CLEVELAND – The Man of Peace

and took out the velvet bag. I took the bag to the bedroom and closed the door.

The diamonds glistened as I dumped them onto the bed. I got the bag of fake diamonds from the bag on the floor by the bed and opened them. To the untrained eye it would be impossible to tell the fakes from the real diamonds. I put half of the real diamonds back into the velvet bag, and poured what looked like an equal amount of the fake ones in a pile next to the real ones.

When I was satisfied that I had gotten the right amount of fakes and real diamonds together I sat looking at the pile. I took the diamonds from the bag and put them into a sock. After I stashed the sock with my clothes I put the mixture of fake and real diamonds into the velvet bag.

I went back to the bar and put the velvet bag back into the box. I heard Darryl coming in from the patio so I poured myself a drink, so it wouldn't look suspicious. When he came into the room I offered him a drink.

"No, brother I am done with all of that," he said as he came and sat by the bar.

"Well, I'll drink for you bro. Here's to hitting the road," I said as I sipped the drink. There was no turning

CLARK KENT

back now. The switch had been made and I was ready to go.

"Thanks big bro! This really means a lot to me," I said as we walked back outside. Jimmy pulled up ten minutes later in a metallic blue conversion van. It had gold pinstripes down the sides and it sat on 22 inch gold rims. Across the top of the windshield gold sticker letters said: *Saints shoutin' in the night.*

"Damn! This is yo van bro?" I asked as he walked out to meet Jimmy in the drive way.

"That's my baby!" he said smiling. The sliding door opened and Sam climbed out of the side of the van.

"That's a nice van dude," Sam said as he reached out to shake Darryl's hand. The driver's side door opened and Jimmy got out of the van.

"Nephew a ride like that makes me want to invest in a fleet of custom vans. You got that baby hooked up," he said as he came to greet us.

"Did you get a chance to hear that system?" Darryl asked as he walked to the driver's side of the van. He reached inside and turned on the radio. It sounded like a concert. Bass reverberated hard enough to feel it from outside of the van. The system had a crisp clear sound to it.

I walked over and looked into the sliding door. There were two captain's chairs and a bed in the back. There was even a refrigerator and a sink. The backs of the chairs all had little T.V. screens on them. It was one of the coldest vans I had ever seen.

White lights lined the inside of the van. As the music played it looked like the lights were dancing to the music.

"Damn bro we rollin in style huh?" I asked as I walked around the van. It looked like it should be in a car show. The interior and exterior were in mint condition. The engine was strong and had a deep sound rumbling from the tail pipes.

"This is my church van. It was donated to us by a man who has a Christian radio show back in Cleveland. We use it for when the choir performs at different places," Darryl said as he turned the van off. We all stood in front of the van for a minute talking, and then went inside. Uncle Jimmy and I had a couple of shots of some of his special stash of fine Scotch. Jimmy told me that he had put my car in storage to keep it off of the streets while I was gone.

CLARK KENT

Monique called and told us she was on her way with the money. We said our final goodbye's and went out to wait for Monique to meet us out by the van.

"Bro this is about to be a fun road trip," Darryl said as we climbed into the van. Monique pulled up and parked in front of the van. She got out and came to the side of the van. She opened the sliding door and got inside.

"Wow! This looks like some rappers tour bus," she said once she was inside. She reached into her bra and pulled out a wad of cash. "I put a little more with it to make sure you're good till you get back," she said as I spun my chair around to face her.

Her eyes were watery and she came to sit on my lap. She traced my face with her fingers. She looked like she was loosing her best friend.

"Be careful daddy! Don't forget about me, and don't go back on the promise you made me. I'll be waiting for you. You better call me every night. Do you hear me?" she asked with her head on my shoulder.

"I'll be back baby. And then we can live the life we need to. Everything will be fine. I'll call you every chance I get baby," I said as I kissed her cheek.

YELLOW CLEVELAND – The Man of Peace

"Goodbye Darryl it was nice to meet you," she said as she opened the door and got out of the van. As she walked away I felt sadness in my heart. I hoped that it wasn't the last time I would ever see her.

"Well, you ready bro?" Darryl asked as he turned on the van.

"I'm ready bro let's roll!" I said as he shifted into gear and pulled off. There was no turning back now. We were on our way back to Cleveland.

Chapter 10

Road Trip

We were rolling across the country on Route 66 - a ride that gives you an opportunity to really let you see the country. The van was like a plush hotel room on wheels. The sound system was top notch. Because the van was a church van we had no problems with police or any kind of highway patrol.

Our first stop was in Arizona. We had been driving nonstop for almost five hours. We pulled in to a city called Flagstaff. And found a restaurant called The Brix. I had always imagined Arizona as a hot place, but as we got out of the van it felt like Cleveland weather. It was freezing.

After a steak dinner and wine we were back on the road again. We drove pretty much straight through from there. I climbed into the bed in the back of the van and stretched out.

My mind drifted to thoughts of everything that had happened in California. I felt like I had been saved from an almost certain death. The diamonds had killed my cousin and his girl. If I had stayed it would've eventually put me in the middle of an all out war.

I laughed to myself thinking about the fact that a church van was sent to bring me back to Cleveland. My big brother had become a minister and he had really changed. He truly was a believer now. It was like God had used angels to pull it all off.

I had once again got out of the city with a large amount of cash. On top of that my bank account was ridiculous. I lit a joint and lay back watching a movie. It was *The Mack* ironically. Watching the movie brought back memories of times on Sunset. It was a trip to think that all these years later there were still real pimps and hoes out there.

Cleveland was different though. There was no track where pimps hung out watching over their hoes. The mentality was different in Cleveland not to mention the weather. I had gotten used to the hot summers in California and Las Vegas.

I remembered how much it used to snow in Cleveland. Of course it was the beginning of spring now and the weather would be nice. In all actuality spring and

YELLOW CLEVELAND – The Man of Peace

summer were the best times to be in Cleveland. People in Cleveland worshipped the warm parts of the year.

I remembered how the smell of BBQ grills filled the air as people got together for family reunions in the parks. Euclid Creek would be full of families enjoying the great outdoors. As I lay there reminiscing I drifted off to sleep with thoughts of Cleveland dancing through my head.

I was back at the mall with Ricky. We were standing in line at S'barro's pizza. As I looked around at the people in the food court I was frozen in time. With each face I saw was a person I had dealt with in the past. I saw Dawn dressed in a beautiful white sundress. Ricky handed me a roll of money and told me to pay for the pizza and then walked away. I stood frozen as a group of boys ran past me. I got the pizza and sat at a table. Just as I sat down I heard gun shots coming from the direction of the restrooms.

Ricky emerged from the crowd running full speed in my direction. He raised his gun and started shooting at me. A bullet hit me in the chest and knocked me to the floor. I was going to die.

I jumped up and opened my eyes. I had been dreaming. I looked at my chest and saw that there was

CLARK KENT

no blood. I was in the back of my brother's van safe and on my way to Cleveland. Darryl had the music thumping and we were rolling full speed in the middle of the night.

I fell back asleep. Now I was in Forest Hills Park; walking with Dawn. She had on the same housekeeper's outfit that she was wearing when I saw her in Vegas. We were adults now and she seemed wiser and stronger.

She reached her hand out for me to grab. As I reached for her I suddenly felt like she was drifting away from me. As if she was on a boat in water being carried out by the tide. Her eyes had filled with tears and she stared at me crying.

"How could you do this to me?" she said as she slowly disappeared from sight. I looked around and found myself standing in an alley. I could see something sticking out from the lid of a garbage dumpster.

I walked towards the dumpster and lifted the lid. The body of a young woman who had been butchered and cut beyond recognition lay in the dumpster on top of bags of trash. As I looked closer I saw that it was Jersey. My heart skipped a beat. I had never wanted to see her that way. I had neglected to watch her back and allowed her to be killed.

YELLOW CLEVELAND – The Man of Peace

When I woke up we were parked at a truck stop. Darryl was asleep in the front seat. The sun was rising and we had a perfect view of the sunrise. I got out of the van and went into the store. I bought a bottle of Hennessy and a pack of cigarettes. I walked back to the van and looked inside. Darryl was still knocked out so I decided to sit and watch the sunrise while I polished of the bottle and smoked.

As I watched the sunrise I thought about Monique. If her baby came out looking like me it would probably ruin her marriage. In a way I felt like it was more her fault than mine. She had neglected to tell me that she had a husband until it was too late.

I climbed back into the van and put on another movie. As I laid there I realized how tired I really was. I finished the Hennessy and stretched out. Before I knew it, I had drifted off to sleep again.

I dreamed that we had gotten back on the road. We had pulled into a truck stop for gas. I got out of the van and walked into a restaurant. An older white lady smiled as I entered the restaurant. As I walked through the restaurant I entered what looked like the "Wal-Mart" of truck stops. There were aisles and aisles of travel goods.

CLARK KENT

Everything, you could possibly need from aspirin to zoo animals.

I was buzzed. As I walked through the store I couldn't help but notice how friendly these white people were. Everyone that I walked past seemed to be in the happiest of moods. It was as if white people had never had any kind of problem with black people.

As I approached the front of the store a big guy wearing a biker vest walked in front of me like I didn't even exist. He walked to the register and pulled a pistol from his jacket.

"Get the fuck down bitches!" he yelled as he shot the gun in the air. I looked around and saw that people had started to scatter in every direction.

Before I could react I was grabbed from behind by another guy also wearing a biker vest and carrying a shotgun. I was pushed to the ground and hit with the butt of the shotgun. I fell to the ground and was immediately pinned down by a boot to the neck.

The big guy who had pulled out his pistol had the gotten the cashier to open the cash register and was motioning for the guy with the shotgun to move. As soon as he started to run a burst of gunshots came from the

YELLOW CLEVELAND – The Man of Peace

direction of the restaurant. Glass shattered from shelves as the bullets sprayed the aisle.

I jumped up and noticed that I had been having another crazy dream. Darryl was listening to a Christian hip hop song and was driving at least ten miles over the speed limit. He sped around a semi truck and switched lanes again once he had passed it.

"I was wondering how it was possible for you to sleep with me banging this new group called *First Unity*," he said as I moved to the front of the van. It was 5:00 am and we were on Interstate 71. We were inside of the Ohio state line.

"Damn bro where the in hell are we?" I asked as I sat in the front passenger seat.

"We just passed Cincinnati. We are about four hours away from home bro," he said as he turned the radio down. I rolled down the window to smell the freshness of the trees. "I want you to check out these young brothers from the church," he said as he pressed a button on the CD player.

The song started off with a recording of a speech by Dr. Martin Luther King. A drum beat started and the bass made the van shake. A girl with a pretty voice started to sing.

CLARK KENT

"*I guess I just can't win. Caught up in this life of sin, I need to be born again...*" Her voice was strong and she sang with conviction. The music played behind her in perfect rhythm to her words. The voice of a gangster rapper caught my attention because he sounded like he should be on a 2 Pac album instead of a spiritual hip-hop song. His voice reminded me of Scarface.

"*It wasn't always easy, but God was always there to pull me through and I can call on God when there's no one in the world for me to turn to. Some say that God is love in times of hate. The light in the dark, the ruler of fate. God is great! I thank God for daily bread, two arms, two legs, and a head. I was blessed this morning to be able to get out of bed.*"

The rapper had a voice that seemed to touch my soul. His voice made it easy to feel the realness in his words. He was rapping about God. Not the God that we all argue over. His words spoke of the all true real God.

As I sat there listening to this new form of positive rap, I felt like I was standing with God. The next verse came on and it felt like it was from my own heart.

"*Bis Mi llah! And praise to the creator of this earth and human birth, upon a star. Allah hu Akbar! Why? Cause he makes the sun rise, and plus yo eyes see. I praise Allah cause he created you, and created me. Some people pray when they in jail, until they get out. Go to church on Sunday but Monday they go and hit out...."*

I had never heard anyone rap about God and sound so true and hard. I continued to listen and I knew that I needed to hear this song again.

"Wow bro! Those dudes went off on that song!" I said as I reached to start the song over. We were almost to Columbus and I was listening to the song for the tenth time when Darryl pulled into a rest stop.

Chapter 11
Coming Home

"A lot has changed since the last time you were home bro. Not just the city, but the people as well. East Cleveland is now basically a war zone. Everybody has moved to the outskirts of the city. Cleveland Clinic has bought up almost the entire lower east side," Darryl said as he pulled into a parking space near the restrooms. As he turned off the van he looked at me as if what he was about to say was going to blow my mind.

"Mama and Pops have also done some changing since you left," he said as he got out of the van.

"What's that supposed to mean?" I asked as I got out of the van and walked towards him.

"You're not going to believe this Jace, but they have become Muslims," he said as he leaned on the front of the van. He was right I couldn't believe what he had told me. The last thing I remembered was Mama taking us to church every Sunday. My Dad never really got into

CLARK KENT

religion much either, so for them to have become Muslims a lot had definitely changed.

"Wow I guess you're right, it sounds like a lot has changed. I mean first you show up as a preacher, and now you're telling me that they are Muslims. Next you're going to tell me that Amy is a Nun," I said as I lit a cigarette.

"No, she's still Amy. She is still Daddy's little princess, who can do no wrong only now she's almost eighteen," he said as he reached into his pocket for his cigarettes. We sat in silence for a few minutes as we smoked. I couldn't believe so much time had past since I had left Cleveland. I was barely eighteen years old myself when I decided to go and visit my big cousin Charles.

"Damn bro I'm really going to miss Smooth. He really looked out for me out there. We were more like brothers than cousins," I said as I thumped my cigarette into the grass.

"Speaking of brothers, I almost forgot that you have never seen your baby brother Doc. He's turning nine soon. That boy has a voice. When he comes to the church he always gets standing ovations," he said as he stretched out his arms and let out a yawn.

"Is he in the choir or something?" I asked.

YELLOW CLEVELAND – The Man of Peace

"No, we have talent nights every second Saturday of the month. We get some of the local kids and teenagers to rap, sing, and dance. I bet you'd turn it out. Do you still rap?" he asked.

"Man I'm still the coldest. I still kick a little freestyle from time to time. I don't really think any of my flows would be suitable for church though, I rap about the streets," I told him. He laughed as we walked into the restrooms. It was going to be a trip having a little brother. I was no longer the baby of the family. Maybe my parents would finally stop treating me like a baby now I thought as I walked to the sink to wash my hands.

Someone in one of the stalls was grunting and groaning like they were in labor. As I turned to walk out the sound of a cell phone ringing caught my attention.

"Hello, hey listen boss, I haven't seen the preacher and the thief at all and I'm almost to Cleveland. What if they are still out there somewhere lying low?" the voice of the person who had been grunting and groaning asked from inside the stall. I looked at my brother who had heard it too. We decided to hurry to the van and follow the car when the Italian came out of the restroom. It was kind of like the hunter being chased by the game now.

CLARK KENT

A big Italian looking guy came out of the restroom and walked to a late model Cadillac. We noticed that there was another guy in the passenger seat of the Cadillac.

"Those bitches have probably been right behind us the whole way. I wonder if they even knew who they were looking for," I said as we watched the Cadillac pull off.

"That's good because now we have the drop on them. They must've been looking for somebody dressed as a preacher," Darryl said as he pulled out of the rest area a few cars behind the Cadillac.

"What do you think we should do?" I asked.

"We are going to have to do this like Marines and circumvent," Darryl said.

"What is that supposed to mean?" I asked as I took the half eaten burger from my Burger King bag.

"It means we have to plan it out as we go along. Right now we have the advantage. It's like Angels came down and led us to that bathroom. If I hadn't wanted to stop for a smoke we never would've known that anyone was even looking for us," Darryl explained.

YELLOW CLEVELAND – The Man of Peace

"I don't think Angels had anything to do with you having a cigarette bro," I said as I devoured the remainder of my burger. We both laughed and Darryl rolled down the windows. He reached for his pack of cigarettes and lit one up. Once I had finished my burger I followed suit.

The Cadillac was moving pretty fast but Darryl stayed with them driving a few cars behind them. I was beginning to wonder if these Italians would ever stop chasing me but as long as we kept following them I knew we were ahead of the game.

I turned on the radio to listen to the Christian rap that I had developed a liking for. As I listened I noticed that the lyrics were like a prayer. The rappers had found a way to pray to the beat.

I had listened to the CD so much that I found myself singing along. As I repeated the lyrics I felt like I was praying instead of just rapping. After following the Cadillac for about an hour and a half it turned off onto an exit ramp. We kept following them only now there were no other cars between us and them.

The Cadillac pulled into a gas station and the two Italians got of the car and walked inside. We pulled into a parking space at the far end of the parking lot, facing

CLARK KENT

the entrance to the gas station. As we sat waiting for them to come back out an idea hit me.

I got out of the van and slowly walked to the Cadillac. I pulled out my switch blade and slashed the back tire on the driver's side of the car. I walked back to the van laughing to myself.

"I'm not sure that was really the best idea Jace," Darryl said as I got into the van.

"Why do you say that? Now they won't be able to look for us," I told him.

"Well, first of all they might get suspicious and know that we've spotted them. Second of all now we'll have to hurry up and get back on the road and once again it will be them who are following us," Darryl said with a frustrated look on his face.

I pulled out my cell phone and called Uncle Jimmy. He answered on the first ring, and I could hear music in the background.

"Hello, this is Jimmy," he said as he seemed to have turned down the music.

"Hey Uncle, what's the good word?" I asked.

"Well nephew your worries are over. I personally talked to the Italians and returned the diamonds. As of

YELLOW CLEVELAND – The Man of Peace

about six hours ago all is forgiven," Uncle Jimmy said. I knew he was lying but I pretended to believe him.

"We're almost in Cleveland," I told him as I climbed into the back of the van to find my duffle bag.

"Okay well stay out of trouble out there. Hey listen, I have some important business to tend to. I have some clients with me and I need to get back to business. I'll give you a call later," he said just before he hung up the phone.

I opened my duffle bag and pulled out the chrome plated revolver that I usually kept with me. I put it in my waistband. As I climbed back into the front seat I saw that Darryl was on the phone as well. Whoever he was talking to had agreed to meet up with us as soon as we got into the city.

"Who was that?" I asked.

"That was someone else who has done a lot of changing since you last saw him. I know you remember Big Ricky from back in the day. Well, when he came home from prison he was also Muslim. His name is now Yaseen. He has a lot of influence with the younger Muslims and he is going to help us get rid of the Italians," he said.

CLARK KENT

I was really shocked now. The last time I had seen Ricky was when he ran past me in the mall and threw the pistol which was now in my waistband, into my lap. I thought back to the money he had handed to me. It was that money that had helped me to start a new life in California. It was crazy to think of seeing him again.

"He actually helps us with the youth of our congregation. He has a program called Pass it Down. He helps the youngsters stay out of gangs and gang violence. All of the leaders of the gangs respect him. He even has some of them come to the community center and talk to the youngsters about how dangerous gangs can be," he explained.

"How do you have Muslims and gang bangers coming to a church?" I asked.

"Our church is non denominational. That means we welcome everybody. Our message is that it's not how you pray, it's that you pray," he said as he took an off ramp onto I-480. We were almost within city limits now. I felt a sense of nostalgia as soon as I saw the sign that said we were inside of the Bedford city limits. Ten minutes later the city skyline became visible and I knew I was finally home.

Chapter 12
Grace and Forgiveness

It was crazy seeing the city after so many years. We got off of the freeway on 55th street. It didn't really look like much had changed at all. The first stop we made was at the Marathon gas station where there was a deli that sold some of the best corned beef sandwiches in the city.

"Man, I haven't had a corned beef sandwich in year's bro," I said as I climbed out of the van.

"We're supposed to be hooking up with Yaseen and some of his homeboys here, but you're right I could go for a corned beef sandwich too," Darryl said as he walked into the deli. The smell of corned beef was like heaven to my nose. I ordered a jumbo sized sandwich with extra pickles.

While we were waiting for our sandwiches a van pulled up behind our van and six huge men dressed in Muslim garments got out of the van and came into the deli. Immediately I noticed Ricky. He had gotten a lot

CLARK KENT

bigger but his face still looked the same. As soon as he saw me his face lit up with a smile.

"As-Salaam-u-Alaikum my brother," he said as he gave me a big brotherly hug.

"Damn man you look like you ate all of the food they had in jail," I told him.

"You look good brother; I guess you must've used that head start I gave you wisely," he said as he looked me up and down. I almost got mad and asked how he thought his head start could've really been a good thing, but I decided to let it go.

"Let's just say I didn't spend it all in one place," I said with a grin.

"It's good to see you man, let me introduce you to the rest of the brothers," he said as he motioned for me to follow him back outside. When we got out to the van I noticed that there were a few other familiar faces. After all of the introductions were made Yaseen and Darryl went back into the deli to get the food. When they came back out Yaseen got into the van with us and the rest of the brothers got into the other van.

We drove to Darryl's house which was on 112th and Superior. Driving up Superior brought back all sorts of memories. I remembered when I had gotten beaten by the police and thrown out of their car at the lake. Then I remembered how much I used to like going to Mr. T's fish store to see all of the aquariums when I was a kid.

While we were driving Darryl told Yaseen about the diamond heist and the Italians who had been after me. He told us that he had some connections in Little Italy who could tell him if there was any real threat. We all knew that the Italians wouldn't dare to come into a black neighborhood looking for anybody.

After Darryl checked his voicemail we left and went to go see my parents. They had moved out to Maple Heights a suburb on the Far East side. We drove up Superior past our old house on Superior Hill. As we drove the nostalgia was amazing. I thought about my high school sweetheart Dawn, and how we used to walk through Forest Hill Park after school.

Yaseen told me that his sister had three kids and was still living in East Cleveland. He said that she was still into thugs and had gotten pregnant while he was in jail. He said that she was doing okay although he didn't like the father of her children.

"Why did you hand me that money and toss that gun in my lap?" I asked.

CLARK KENT

"Man... that was along time ago... That was definitely a day I wish that I could take back. I went to the mall that day to end a beef with a big time dope boy from East Cleveland. I had robbed a guy that everybody called Tuffy. I was supposed to be paying back the money; but I changed my mind when we were in the car smoking weed. I didn't know how it was all going to play out until the last second. I knew that nobody would think that some young kid had the gun and the money and I figured that you would have a better chance of getting away than I did. That's why I left the money with you. I figured I was paying you to get rid of the gun," he said as we turned onto Lee road.

"I was scared as hell! I ended up hiding the gun and the money in the park. Eventually I went back and got it. The funny thing is that believe it or not I still have that pistol," I told him. I opened up my bag and pulled out the chrome plated 38 revolver that I had kept with me the whole time. I had gotten kind of attached to it.

"Wow, I never would have guessed that you would still be carrying that damn gun. The only reason I beat that case was because the cops never found the murder weapon," he said as I handed him the gun. He looked at it and opened the barrel. After he spun the barrel he slammed it shut and handed it back to me. "I have no use for this anymore. I have given my life to Allah. I pray that one day you'll do the same. In the mean time you need to throw that thing in the lake somewhere," he said. I wiped the gun clean and put it back into my bag.

"How do you go from being a hustler to being a Muslim?" I asked.

"Only by the grace and forgiveness of Allah, my brother," he replied. We rode the rest of the way to my parent's house in silence. I couldn't help but to laugh to myself about it now that I was back in Cleveland.

My parent's house was beautiful. Dad had done most of the work himself. The front yard had two small apple trees and a grapevine growing over the fence. There was a small pond in the middle of the yard with rose bushes growing around it.

Before we could get to the door my father came out of the house wearing a long white robe and sandals. He wore the traditional white beanie that Muslims wear. He looked very happy. As soon as he saw me he smiled and greeted me much the same way as Yaseen had, then he greeted Yaseen and Darryl.

"As-Salaam-u-Alaikum son. Your mother has been waiting for you all day long. Let's go inside. Are you

CLARK KENT

brother's hungry? She made something short of a feast for you," he said as he led us into the house.

The living room was decorated with beautiful paintings that my Dad had painted himself. Plants hung in pots in the corners and smaller plants grew on different shelves that I could tell my dad had also made himself. On a coffee table there was a fancy chess set. My parents still had exquisite taste when it came to home decor.

"Oh Allah! I can't believe my baby is finally home," my mother said as she rushed over and gave me the biggest hug ever. She had on a lavender robe with beautiful designs and her head was covered with a white scarf that had lace trim. Her face seemed to have a glow. I would have never guessed that she would be a Muslim. I didn't even know white people could become Muslims.

"Get yourselves washed up I have a wonderful meal for us," she said as she went into the kitchen. I followed Darryl and Yaseen and we washed our hands and faces. Yaseen explained the traditional way to wash up before meals and prayers. He called it making wudu. After we were done washing up my father led us to a room in the back of house.

YELLOW CLEVELAND – The Man of Peace

We sat on the floor around a huge dish in the middle of the room. There was meat, rice, and pita bread along with fruits, and vegetables. I had never seen people eat like this before. Everyone ate from the same dish using only their hands and the pita bread. I must admit I was very intrigued.

Once we were done eating my mother came in and cleared away the empty dish. She brought in a large bowl of water and we all washed our hand again. My father pulled out a large book with gold print and Arabic writing on the cover.

He opened the book and began reading a story to us about God's forgiveness. I sat there listening to the story and I began to understand my parent's newfound sense of happiness. This was all new to me but I found it all very interesting. When my father finished reading the story he said a prayer and began explaining to me what he called the pillars of Islam.

This was the first time I had ever seen my father so serious about religion. It was like he had somehow seen the light so to speak. When he was finished he asked me if I would recite some kind of prayer in Arabic with him.

"Repeat, after me," he said. "La illaha ilAllah. (There is no God but God)." Even though I didn't quite

CLARK KENT

understand what he was saying I felt a sense of relief go through my body. We talked for a little while longer and then Darryl told my father we had to go and take care of some important business. I hugged my mother and kissed her cheek and then we left.

Chapter 13
Loose Ends

The one thing I hadn't told anybody was that I had kept nearly half of the diamonds. It was also how I knew Uncle Jimmy was lying when he said he had returned the diamonds to the Italians. They would have immediately noticed that half of the diamonds had been replaced with fake diamonds and probably would have killed him on the spot the same way they did Pretty Tony.

I did know that I would be safe now that I had made it back to Cleveland. I had found out that my sister Amy had gone away to college so I knew that the Italians were bluffing when they said they knew where she lived. Another thing that gave me a sense of relief was my newfound connection with the Muslims in Cleveland.

I had done Yaseen a huge favor by keeping the gun out of harms way. He in turn had given me the money that had been both my way out as well as my start up money for my illegal business ventures over the years.

CLARK KENT

I was back in Cleveland with enough money to start over in my bank account, as well, as almost a half million dollars worth of stolen diamonds. The only person who knew about the bank account was Uncle Jimmy. He had given me $200,000 for the heist. He was supposed to have split the money with my cousin Smooth, but when Smooth and his girl were killed he had changed the deal and low balled me.

It was crazy to think that after all of the craziness that had happened I had still ended up with some of the diamonds. I had given them to Pretty Tony and thought that would be the end of it. I still didn't know how Jimmy had gotten them back but he had set me up to take the fall for the heist just as I knew he would which is why I had stolen half of the diamonds. In a way I felt bad about stealing the diamonds but after everything that I had gone through I almost felt entitled to some of them.

As we rode back into the city I wondered how I would sell the diamonds. After thinking about it I decided to wait for the right time and ask Big Ricky, or as he was now known as Yaseen if he could help me. I had decided that if he could help me find a buyer for the diamonds I would give him a cut of the money.

YELLOW CLEVELAND – The Man of Peace

We were driving back into the city when out of no where the van started to overheat. The radiator had sprung a leak and now we were stranded on the side of the road on interstate 480. Darryl had pulled over to the side of the road and we were in a bad situation. For one thing I had the diamonds, and if we couldn't get the van started before the police found us we would have been caught with a dirty pistol and a half a million dollars worth of stolen diamonds.

Yaseen got out of the van and spread out a small rectangular rug on the ground. He was carrying some sort of beads. He stood in front of the rug and put his hands to his ears then closed his eyes and started praying in some other language. Next he knelt down and did some sort of a bow.

I had never seen a Muslim pray before. I decided that I wanted to learn more about Islam one day but right now I was praying that the police didn't show up. Yaseen was right; I needed to get rid of that gun as soon as possible. Darryl was on the phone calling a tow truck. When Yaseen was finished with his prayer he whispered something over each shoulder and sat looking at his beads as if he were counting them.

CLARK KENT

A tow truck was passing by and had pulled over in front of the van. A heavy set older white man climbed out of the truck and asked if we needed help. Darryl was still on the phone trying to get a tow truck and he hadn't even noticed what was going on. I walked over and explained what was going on, and the tow truck driver quickly hooked the van up to the tow truck.

We all got into the van and were towed to an auto repair shop in Garfield Heights. While we waited for the van to be fixed Yaseen explained to me that the prayer rug is where the stories of the magic carpet had come from. He said that during the time of the prophet Muhammad, the people's belief was so strong that often their prayers would be answered before they could even finish praying. It was as if the prayer rug were a magic carpet.

When the van was ready we paid the mechanic and were on our way. I thought about my parents and how happy they looked. I decided to show Darryl and Yaseen the diamonds and see if we could find a fence for them. Darryl didn't want anything to do with them. Yaseen said he would ask around and see if he could find a buyer but he really didn't want to deal with them either. It was beginning to look like I was going to be stuck with them for the time being.

YELLOW CLEVELAND – The Man of Peace

Being back in Cleveland I needed a car. I had Darryl take me a used car lot so I could look around and see if I could find something classy. I needed to be rolling in style again. In Cleveland appearances were everything. I decided on a Cadillac El Dorado. After a quick test drive I wrote a check for the full price of the car and we were on our way.

I told Darryl I would meet up with him in a few hours. I wanted to go shopping for some new clothes to go with my new ride. It felt great being able to buy anything I wanted and I couldn't wait until I went out for a night on the town feeling like a new man.

Chapter 14
Dirty Laundry

After a bit of a shopping spree I decided to go visit my parents again. I wanted to hear more about what had changed their lives so much. When I walked into the house I was hit with a sense of de ja vu. The smell of garlic and spaghetti sauce hit my nose and immediately I felt like I was thirteen years old coming home after school to my mother's famous spaghetti. As I stood in the entryway my mind flashed to visions of my father sitting with a friend in front of the chess board.

I was brought back to reality as my baby brother walked into the room. It was like looking at a mirror. He was carrying a book bag and wearing headphones.

"What's up Doc?" he asked as he took off his headphones.

"Wow look at you man. I can't believe it took so long for us to finally meet," I said as I reached out to hug him.

"Mom and Pops have told me all about you. My big brother, the adventurer," he said as we walked into the

CLARK KENT

kitchen. When we walked in Mama put down her wooden spoon and rushed over to hug me.

"I made your favorite! I have some garlic bread in the oven and I even got iced tea. You always loved iced tea," she said as she looked up into my eyes. Mama was short so quite naturally I was taller than her. "I can see the travel in your eyes; my baby has definitely been on an adventure. Go get washed up and get ready for dinner. Doc go out back and tell your father Jason is here," she said as she took the bread out of the oven. It definitely felt good to be home again.

When I walked into the bathroom my little brother was using the same method of washing up that Pops and Yaseen use before prayer. He let the water fill his hands, and then splashed it over his face. Then he swished his mouth out. Even though he was only nine years old he had the routine down pat.

When he was done I washed up the same way as he had and then I headed out to the back yard to see Pops. He was pitching horse shoes with my Uncle Billy. It had been years since I had seen anybody pitching horse shoes.

"What's up Pops? Wow Uncle Billy too? This is like a family reunion," I said as I walked out of the house into

YELLOW CLEVELAND – The Man of Peace

the backyard. Uncle Billy was my absolute favorite uncle. When we were kids he'd always ask me if I had a dollar. If I said "no" he would grab my hand and tell me that every man has to have at least a dollar at all times, then he'd reach into his pocket and give me a dollar.

"Is that you Diablo?" Uncle Billy always called me Diablo. He said it meant devil in Spanish. "You got a dollar boy?" he asked as he stretched out his arms to hug me.

"I definitely got me a dollar," I told him.

"Boy you look good nephew! How's the world? Is it still out there Diablo?" he asked as he looked me over.

"It's still out there, and of course the game hasn't changed. It's still every dog for his self out there," I said as I sat down at the picnic table. Pops and Uncle Billy came and sat down too. We sat catching up a bit and talking about my time in California. As we were talking I heard a voice singing in what sounded like Arabic. It was my baby brother Doc singing the Muslim call to prayer.

He had a beautiful singing voice. The way he sang made the song sound like a poem. Pops and Uncle Billy got up and went inside to wash up for prayer. By the time Doc was finished Pops had the prayer rugs laid out and was beginning to speak in Arabic. Uncle Billy and Doc stood side by side behind Pops so I joined in.

Pops had really learned the prayers. He was speaking so fast it was hard to believe he was reciting scriptures straight out of the Koran. We went through all of the same prostrations I had seen Yaseen doing when he was praying. When my father was done praying; he whispered something over his left shoulder then whispered something over his right shoulder.

I thought that we were done praying, but I wondered why no one had gotten up yet. I peeked at my father and saw that his hands were in sort of a cup formation. He sat mumbling something that I couldn't hear. After almost five whole minutes of silence He appeared to be splashing his face with water the way we did while washing up only this time there wasn't any water.

After prayer we all sat in a circle and listened to Pops read from a thick green book. He read a story about the prophet Muhammad. Every time he said the Prophet's name he said something in Arabic that he said meant; may God's blessings be with him. When he was finished with the story we all got up and went out into the back yard.

YELLOW CLEVELAND – The Man of Peace

Everything that I had seen had blown my mind. I wondered again what had caused such a transformation in the lives of my parents. They seemed so at peace, I wondered if I would ever be so at peace myself.

We talked for a while and I told my father about what had happened to Smooth and his girlfriend. My father already knew most of it, but he didn't know that Uncle Jimmy was the one who had actually set it all up. When I told him I could tell that it had really upset him.

He told me that he and Uncle Jimmy had fallen out years ago over a very similar situation. He didn't go into details about it, but he told me that Uncle Jimmy was not really someone who could be trusted when it came to money. I wanted to show Pops the diamonds but I knew he would be upset that I had further tangled myself into the situation that had already gotten my cousin killed.

Uncle Jimmy was my mother's brother. I didn't even know that he and Pops had ever even really dealt with each other. Uncle Billy had never met Uncle Jimmy but I could tell that he had some mixed feelings about him. Uncle Billy was my father's older brother so if something made Pops mad, Uncle Billy was going to take the side of his younger brother.

CLARK KENT

I stayed at my parent's house until after dinner. There was no way I was going to miss my favorite meal. After dinner I told my parents that I was going to let my little brother hang out with me so we could get to know each other. My mother refused to let me leave without taking a meatball sub for the road, and I had no problem taking it either.

Once I was in the car I called Darryl. He told me to meet him at his apartment. Yaseen had learned that there were people looking for me in connection with the diamonds. The situation had once again caught up with me. The time had come to deal with this dirty laundry once and for all.

Chapter 15

Meeting the Brothers

I decided to take my little brother shopping for new school clothes before going to Darryl's house. I laughed to myself thinking about how much he reminded me of myself when I was his age. He was very mature, and his conversations didn't seem like the kind of conversations that you would hear from kids his age.

As we were leaving the mall I got a text from Darryl telling me that he had some people at his house who he wanted me to meet. I text him back and told him that I was on my way and that I had Doc with me. I wondered who he wanted me to meet, even though I knew it was most likely someone who was interested in the diamonds. My experience with Darryl had taught me that he always had some kind of motive.

I pulled up in front of his apartment building and reached under my seat for my pistol. I figured it would be better to be safe than sorry. I put the gun in my waistband and turned off the car. Doc looked at me and laughed.

CLARK KENT

"You wont need that gun here big bro. These cars parked in front of us belong to the brothers. That van belongs to Muhammad, and the car in the driveway is Abdul Aziz's," he said as we got out of the car. The door to Darryl's apartment opened before I even got a chance to knock. Inside there were about six or seven people sitting in the living room.

Yaseen stood up and greeted us as we walked in. Right away I noticed some familiar faces. I was introduced to the brothers one by one before I sat down. Abdul Aziz was a friend of mines from elementary school who I knew as Martin. Another of the brothers was one of my old friends from my gang days.

"Well bro, let's get down to business. First of all I can tell you that we can't sell the diamonds in Cleveland. News travels faster than you might think. Some people have been waiting for you to try to get rid of the diamonds here," Darryl said as he closed the blinds.

"Man, how in the world did you get caught up in some mess like this?" Abdul Aziz asked. I knew Adul Aziz by his old gang name Assault. He was known for starting fights. He used to be one of the younger guys who always had drama going on. I would have never imagined him dressed in an all white throbe wearing a

YELLOW CLEVELAND – The Man of Peace

turban. Once again I thought to myself that this new religion really was magic.

"It's a long story; let's just say that I had an interesting time in Vegas."

"I guess the old saying about what happens in Vegas stays in Vegas doesn't apply to diamond heists," Muhammad said as he lit up a blunt laughing.

"I didn't know Muslims smoke weed," I said as he blew out a big cloud of smoke.

"Brother, weed is a plant sent to us from heaven. Especially this weed," he said as he passed me the blunt. He was right too; as I inhaled the blunt the taste was like no other weed that I had ever smoked. Immediately I got light headed, and felt that out of body experience.

"They call that weed Ganz, we get that from Detroit," Abdul Aziz said as I passed him the blunt. I was beginning to like their religion more and more. It shocked me how down to earth everybody seemed. I could tell that it had made a big impact on the black community. It seemed like just about everybody I knew had converted to Islam.

As we sat talking, I thought about the fact that the diamond heist was still haunting me. All I had wanted to do was enjoy a week in Vegas. Instead I had been

CLARK KENT

kidnapped, lost my cousin and his girlfriend, watched a friend of mine get beaten to death, and had to leave town. Of course I had made a lot of money in the process but it didn't seem worth it.

"So what can I do about this situation?" I asked.

"For now you just need to kick back and let us handle it," Darryl said.

"If I were you I would take the diamonds to Detroit and sell em!" Abdul Aziz chimed in.

"No, don't try to sell the diamonds at all right now. If word gets out that you have the diamonds things could get real ugly. Not to mention the fact that we're probably the only people in this city that you can trust. The best thing that you can do is put them somewhere safe and not tell anybody else about any of this," Darryl said.

"We got yo' back bro! You know that I'm not about to let anything happen to you," Yaseen said.

"That's the truth! You're in good hands now brother. Trust me, our Jamaat is big, and we take care of our own brother," Muhammad said.

"The truth is that we all need to come together to get our brothers and sisters back on the right track. It's a

YELLOW CLEVELAND – The Man of Peace

sad fact that thirteen percent of all black males eighteen years and older have already lost their right to vote because they have been convicted of felonies. That means they will never get to be a part of this democracy in which we live. We can no longer just sit back and let the system pick us apart. We need to fight back. Now this mess you're in is your own fault due to the decisions that you have made. Did you know that right now in this country thirty-three percent of all of the black young men between the ages of sixteen and twenty-four are either awaiting trial, in jails or prisons or on probation or parole? We need to get our people together brother, and it has to start now!" As Abdul Aziz spoke I thought back to when I had gone to the mall with Yaseen that day so long ago.

"We're going to help you, and in return you are going to help us! You are going to join our mentoring program and help us redirect our youth. We need to show them that there are avenues to success other than drug dealing, robbery, and killing each other," Darryl said as he stood up and handed me a piece of paper. "This is a program that we have started at the church. We meet every Tuesday and Saturday. We get together and teach young brothers and sisters basic life skills. We teach them that life doesn't have to end in these streets by the

CLARK KENT

hands of their peers. I've been working with the brothers and some other influential people around the city getting people both young and old to come together to try to fix this whole mess that plagues our city," Darryl explained.

"Will you join us brother?" Muhammad asked. "We also have programs at the masjids throughout the city. We go out into the community on Wednesday nights inviting people to come and learn about Islam. All in all I think that we are making a huge impact. I mean don't get me wrong, there is still crime but every day more and more of our young brothers and sisters are joining us in this plight."

"I'm in... I mean how could I say no to something as important as this?" I said as I handed Darryl back the paper.

"Young brother if I may butt in I would like to explain a few things," an older brother who had been sitting quietly said. "It's sad to see what we as a people have become. We have been fooled into destroying everything that we have including each other.

We have forgotten what it means to be a community. We have been tricked into chasing the all mighty dollar, and the money that you're making in the process never even comes back into our communities.

Our neighborhoods used to be self sufficient. We had our own stores, restaurants and businesses. The Mom and Pop stores have been sold to people who don't even live in our communities. We spend our money at stores like Wal-Mart, Sam's club, and Mc Donald's but those companies don't invest in our neighborhoods. Our money leaves the black community and never returns.

We wonder why you young brothers and sisters turn to a life of crime when in reality that's all that we have left. It seems that our youth have forgotten how many people died for our rights. Look how many of our young people don't even exercise their right to vote. We seem to have forgotten that we decide who gets elected into the offices of our government.

When they take away things that our communities need to survive it's because we only go out to vote during major elections. You young brothers need to stop blaming the white man for the state of our communities, and start doing something about it."

Normally I would've thought he was just some crazy old man but what he was saying actually made a lot of sense. I thought about the money I had made over the

CLARK KENT

years and how I could invest some of it into something that would help our communities. I also decided that I would show up at the voting polls every time there was an initiative involving our neighborhoods, and every time someone was running for office. He was right - people had died for our right to vote and it would be disrespectful not to exercise that right.

We sat and talked for a while longer before everybody got up to leave. I hadn't heard anybody sound so convincing in my life. I decided to take my little brother home.

As we drove back through the city looking at street after street where gangs had taken over, I knew that it had been meant for me to meet with the brothers. I wanted to help them make a change not only in our community but across the country.

After I dropped Doc off, I went back to Darryl's. I was exhausted and ready for a good night of sleep. I still couldn't believe I had made it back to Cleveland in one piece.

Chapter 16
Cruising Through the City

I woke up the next morning at Darryl's apartment. Darryl was already gone. Darryl had left me a note saying that he had to go to work at the church and that he had left a key for me to lock up if I left before he got home. I looked at my phone and saw that I had missed calls from Yaseen. When I checked my voicemail he had left a message saying that he wanted me to meet up with him and go to the masjid.

After eating a good breakfast I decided that I wanted to cruise through the old neighborhood. I had been gone for a long time and I wanted to see if any of my old friends were around. I drove through East Cleveland and couldn't believe my eyes. Most of the buildings were boarded up, and looking bad. My old high school had been renovated and now looked more like a prison than a school.

As I drove down Euclid Avenue nostalgia kicked in. I remembered all of the fun I had growing up in these streets. I also remembered all of the trouble I used to get

CLARK KENT

into trying to fit in. I thought about how my dad had gotten me into boxing and how much fun it was going to the gym to work out.

At Euclid and Superior I turned right and headed towards 125th and Superior; a neighborhood that we used to call "Hells Kitchen." I drove past the rapid station which was probably the only new thing other than my old school that I had seen on my drive. The Regional Transit Authority had definitely been making money.

As I sat waiting for the light to change I saw a familiar face. Veronica was sitting at the bus stop with three kids all under the age of ten years old. I pulled to the curb and rolled down the window.

"Hey stranger, do you need a ride?" I asked. She looked up and immediately recognized me.

"Hey! I heard you were back in town," she said as she walked to the car. She opened the door and put her kids in the back seat. Once she had them all buckled in she got into the front seat and gave me a big hug. "This is an old friend of Mommy's from school," she told the kids as we drove off. "Say hello." The children were polite and well dressed. "This is my oldest son Michael, the one in the middle is my daughter Nikki, and the baby

YELLOW CLEVELAND – The Man of Peace

is my son Carlos. Kids this nice man is Jason. We were headed downtown; I hope that's not too far."

"Not at all, I was just cruising around looking at the city. I am supposed to meet up with your brother later but I don't mind taking you. Where downtown do you need to go?"

"I have to go to the welfare building, apparently their father has decided that he doesn't want to pay child support anymore and I need to tell them about his new job. So you ran into Ricky huh? He changed a lot during his stay in prison. He don't eat pork no more and all of that. All he talks about is 'Allah' and the Koran. He thinks he can change the world with all of that Muslim nonsense."

"Yeah we hooked up as soon as I got into town. He seems sincere about being a Muslim; it seems that there is a lot of that going around lately. My whole family is Muslim now," I said as I stopped at the street light on 125th and Superior.

Hells kitchen still looked the same. Graffiti still covered all of the dilapidated buildings. A group of thuggish looking teenagers stood on the corner drinking and smoking weed. I recognized a guy buying drugs from them who I had known back when I used to hang in Hells

CLARK KENT

Kitchen. He looked bad. He apparently had gone from being a drug dealer to being a drug addict. I saw him exchange money for drugs from one of the boys and off he went.

"You were just like those boys Jason. I remember when you were hanging on that same corner. It's a good thing that you were able to get away from all of this mess. How many kids do you have now?" She asked.

"I don't have any kids," I told her. "I guess I have been too busy to really settle down for any of that." As I said it I remembered that she had once been pregnant with my baby when we were in high school. We had decided for her to get an abortion.

"Trust me you don't have to settle down to get somebody pregnant. How many girls have you sent to clinic for abortions?" she asked as she reached into her bag to get a bottle for her baby.

"Only one, I never forgot about it either," I said

"That was a hard decision, and I promised myself that I would never do that again," she said as she reached over the seat and gave the baby the bottle. "I still see your brother Darryl from time to time. I've been trying to get over to his church one Sunday but without a car getting around on Sundays is almost impossible."

YELLOW CLEVELAND – The Man of Peace

When we got to the welfare building I gave her my phone number and told her to call me if she needed a ride home. As I pulled away I watched as she herded her kids up the stairs. In a way I was glad that I had seen her. Seeing her with her kids reminded me of why I had left the city in the first place. She had been a big part of what caused me to get involved in the street life.

I drove back through the city thinking of all of the things that had changed since I had left. I decided to go to Cleveland Heights and see if Coventry was still the same. Coventry was a street filled with stores, coffee shops and restaurants. At the top of the street there was an area filled with tables and benches where people would sit and hang out. I remembered hanging with Aaron on the benches watching people walk up and down the street.

Coventry was known as a hippie area but in actuality it was one of the most diverse places in the city. It was a place where color didn't matter. People were always friendly and there was never any trouble. I parked and went into Arabica, a well known coffee shop that had several different kinds of coffee. I ordered my coffee black with no sugar and took it to go.

CLARK KENT

Not much had changed since I had last seen Coventry. As I sat at one of the tables I watched a group of white kids playing hacky sack. Another group of people sat on the benches smoking cigarettes and talking about politics. An older black man in a suit sat reading the newspaper drinking coffee. He looked like a professor or some kind of school teacher. At the table next to him a guy with long dread locks sat typing on a laptop computer talking to a girl dressed in Gothic looking clothes.

As I sat drinking coffee enjoying the scenery I saw my brother Aaron walking with a briefcase talking on his cell phone. He was wearing a shirt and tie with some expensive looking dress shoes on. At first he didn't notice me but when he got closer he hung up his phone and sat down at my table.

"What's up knuckle head? I heard you were in town," he said as he sat down. "I didn't think I would see you over here in my stomping grounds."

"I had to stop by and see if Coventry was still the same. What's up with you Mr. Professor?"

"Aw man just the same old same old. Still trying to teach these youngsters some rhetoric and keep my classes interesting. You look good bro! Are you staying out of trouble these days?" he asked.

"You know me; I'm just trying to keep my head above water. As far as trouble goes life is life," I told him as I watched a beautiful girl come out of the coffee shop.

"I heard you had some drama out in Cali, I hope you left it there," he said as he opened up his briefcase.

"I'm home now drama free. I didn't have a big enough bag to bring all of that drama with me so I left it all behind. What about you? I know its hard teaching classes with all of those pretty college girls running around trying to flirt for a good grade."

"I'm there to teach, I don't let myself get caught up with the students. I get flirted with some times but I'm too smart to let anything like that jeopardize my career."

"I heard that big bro, I'm glad it's you and not me though. I don't think I could do it. I would probably get caught with my hands in the cookie jar," I said with a laugh. "It's good seeing you though big bro."

"Definitely, so what's on your agenda for the day?" he asked.

"I'm just chillin, enjoying this beautiful spring day. I'm probably going to go hang out with Mom and Pops

CLARK KENT

later, but other than that I'm just rolling around seeing the city."

We sat talking as he began grading papers. I had always known he would be successful. When we were kids I always teased him about being a book worm. Now I envied him and wished I had followed in his footsteps.

Chapter 17

The Change

After I had lunch with Aaron I decided it was time to get rid of the gun that I had been carrying around for all of these years. I drove down Martin Luther King Jr. Boulevard to the lake. I had always liked taking this route to the lake because of the beautiful scenery. The boulevard winded through a long stretch of parks and cultural gardens and ended at Lake Erie's 72nd street marina.

I parked the car and sat looking at the water. I remembered countless picnics and barbeques here growing up. It was also one of the best places to watch the sun set over the lake. I rolled a blunt and grabbed the pistol from under my seat. After I wiped it clean and emptied out the bullets I got out of the car and walked down to the water.

There were huge rocks that lined the waterfront where people often sat looking at the lake. I walked down one of the paths that led to the water and sat on one of the big rocks. I decided that I no longer wanted to

CLARK KENT

live by the gun. After I was sure no one was looking I hurled the gun as far as I could. It landed in the water with a splash about fifty feet from the shore. The lake was pretty deep in this area and I knew the gun would be gone forever.

I lit the blunt and said a silent prayer thanking God that I hadn't been caught with the gun over the years. I knew that I should've gotten rid of the gun years ago but for some reason I had kept it. I thought about the day it had landed in my lap and laughed. That day had changed my life and I was finally closing a chapter of my life that could've been a book.

After I finished the blunt I went back to the car and called Yaseen. He told me that he would meet me at a storefront on 66th and Hough. I wrote down the address and told him I was on my way. I almost wished that I still had the pistol. From what I remembered the Hough area was one of the worst parts of the city. To my surprise the area was nothing like I remembered it.

Abdullah's international was a store that sold Islamic apparel as well as books, and various other items. It was located on the corner of a street filled with newly built houses. There was a large park across the street with an impressive playground and a small pond. The last time I

YELLOW CLEVELAND – The Man of Peace

had been in this part of the city there were projects and liquor stores on every corner, but now it looked like a suburb.

A beautiful sister wearing a white scarf greeted me as I walked into the store. She led me to the back of the store where the brothers were. Yaseen, Abdul Aziz, and Muhammad were sitting and listening to an older brother read from the Koran. I walked in and sat down beside them.

Until now when I thought of Muslims I envisioned brothers dressed in suites and bowties selling *Muhammad Speaks* magazines. These brothers wore turbans and beanies with long shirts called throbes. I found out that these Muslims were different, they were called Sunni Muslims. It was the same religion that Malcolm X had learned about after leaving The Nation of Islam and going to Mecca.

I learned that they prayed five times per day and believed in peace and love for all mankind. I learned that there were Muslims of every race and nationality. They lived by a certain set of principals called the pillars of Islam. As I sat listening to the brother speak I became more and more intrigued about the religion. I now understood why my parents had embraced Islam. I

CLARK KENT

pictured myself giving up the street life and one day becoming a Muslim. As I sat listening to the brother talk I wondered if I could ever even be forgiven for the sins I had committed over the years.

After the brother finished talking my first thought was to ask how a person became Muslim. I wondered if there was some sort of ceremony or something. Instead I decided to wait until we were back in my car and ask Yaseen. The brothers all got up and said there salaams before we left. As I was walking to the doorway the older brother who had been talking stopped me.

"Young brother I can see it in your eyes… You are more than curious. You have many questions that you want to ask but haven't figured out how to ask them. It is not a coincidence that you arrived here today. Allah has sent you to learn more about Islam. The brothers that you are with, all came from the same streets that you have come from.

Allah is merciful and forgiving young brother. Are you ready to take your vow of faith?"

"I don't really know what that means," I replied.

"Islam means total submission to the will of Allah. The word Muslim means one who submits. Do you believe in the oneness of God?" he asked.

"Yes!" I replied.

"Then repeat after me. Ashadu ana La illaha illAllah."

"Ashadu ana La illaha illAllah." I repeated.

"Muhammada Rasulullah."

"Muhammada Rasulullah."

"That means; I bear witness that there is no God but Allah, and the profit Muhammad (peace be upon him) is his messenger. Young brother if you believe this in your heart you have just taken your kalimah shahata, or affirmation of faith. It is as simple as that. Now you must commit to these vows and learn the principals, and pillars of Islam. Insha Allah your new name shall be Ibn Abdul Salaam. It means son of the man of peace. As-Salaam-u-Alaikum my brother. I hope to see you again soon insha Allah. Come to the masjid this evening for prayer and as often as possible. Here is a prayer schedule for you. It lists the five obligatory prayers of the day."

I felt like I had made a decision that would help me to turn my life around. Each of the brothers hugged me and gave me their salaams. The Imam gave me a set of beads and told me that there was a lot he wanted to

CLARK KENT

teach me. As I turned to walk out of the store I looked back and saw him smiling at me.

"By the way, please give my salaams to your parents and your brother Ali. They will be very happy to hear the good news you have for them."

I walked out to the car feeling like a new man. I decided that from this day foreword I would live up to the name; Abdul Salaam (The man of peace).

About the Author

Clark Kent's goal as an author is to entertain as well as educate his audience about life in the streets. He puts lessons and morals into his stories while using real life situations and scenarios to captivate his readers. In the course of telling the story he shows the consequences and repercussions of decisions that are made in every day urban life. The name Clark Kent is in no way to be confused with the fictional character from Superman.

K.E.N.T. is actually an acronym for Keeping Every Novel True to the streets. Born in Cleveland, Ohio Mr. Clark began writing about urban life at a young age. His inspirations for writing include authors like Donald Goins, Ice Berg Slim, James Patterson, and Steven King. His stories are partially fictionalized, yet reflect everyday life from a different point of view.

The Yellow series consist of three novellas. Yellow is the first in the series about a young man living and growing up in America's Urban Ghettos.

The second is called Run! Yellow Las Vegas A story about a Las Vegas trip gone bad.

And finally; Yellow Cleveland The man of peace. Yellow is on the run from the Italian Mafia and finding religion.

Thank you for your support. I hope you enjoy the series. God bless.

YELLOW

CLARK KENT

YELLOW CLEVELAND

THE MAN OF PEACE

CLARK KENT

www.ingramcontent.com/pod-product-compliance
Lightning Source LLC
LaVergne TN
LVHW051603070426
835507LV00021B/2743